Don't Get Hooked

Tobacco Awareness and Prevention Activities

David Cowan

Susanna Palomares

INNERCHOICE Publishing
15079 Oak Chase Court
Wellington, FL 33414

www.InnerchoicePublishing.com

Cover: Linda Thille

ISBN - 10: 1-56499-053-2

ISBN - 13: 978-1-56499-053-2

15079 Oak Chase Court
Wellington, FL 33414

www.InnerchoicePublishing.com

CONTENTS

Introduction

Critical Things to Know

Don't Get Hooked is a new and vital resource for educators who are working to help young people build the skills and develop the strength to avoid becoming hooked on tobacco. It can be the heart of a stand alone tobacco intervention or used as a powerful supplement to strengthen any other program that you may have in place or with which you are working. Because of its ease of use, its activities fit well into either the classroom or into counseling or other groups. High impact, simple to use, and flexibility sum up *Don't Get Hooked.*

Here you'll find current information about this drug and a collection of the best and simplest activities to engage kids in the hard facts about tobacco use while creating the resiliency and determination necessary to avoid getting involved.

Tobacco is a drug and using it leads to addiction. The consequences of tobacco use have been and continue to be the biggest public health concern either directly or indirectly facing every one of us. According to United States Department of Health and Human Services Surgeon General's Report, tobacco use continues to be the chief cause of preventable deaths in the United States. It kills more people every year than AIDS, alcohol, all other drugs, murders, suicides, automobile accidents, and fires *combined* (2004).

Despite this danger, 5000 teens and preteens become regular users of tobacco every single day, and about one third of these children will eventually die a "smoker's death" from cancer, heart disease, or lung disease (USDHHS, 2004). According to Donna Shalala, former Secretary of the Department of Health and Human Services, "That statistic poses an urgent public health challenge and—given that we have at hand numerous strategies proven to be effective—a moral imperative. The deadly impact of tobacco use is painfully clear (USDHHS, 2000).

There are many things that account for this seeming paradox. Chief among them and by far and away the greatest influence remains the enormous number of dollars the tobacco industry annually pours into advertising its deadly products. This number jumped from $5.7 billion in 1999 to over $11.2 billion in (USDHHS, 2004). Even with legislation and litigation having put a theoretical damper on the impact of this huge advertising effort, the truth is that *today's ads are designed to get people to start smoking, and more specifically, to get more children involved with tobacco at as early an age as possible.*

Understanding the continuing reality of media influences, *Don't Get Hooked* devotes a whole section to creating awareness of how the tobacco industry marshals its resources to manipulate kids into taking that first step down the road to tobacco (drug) addiction and the deadly promise it holds in store.

By now you have probably noticed that we talk about tobacco use and not just smoking. Although smoking is the chief villain in the world of tobacco users, it certainly isn't alone. What has euphemistically been called "smokeless" tobacco (really chewing or spit tobacco) also leads to addiction and disease. Again, despite the dangers, about 16 percent of boys in grades 9 through 12 are regular users of spit tobacco. That's about one in six, and the number is rising (USDHHS, 2004).

Looking at the problem of tobacco use from another perspective, consider that over 90 percent of today's adult tobacco users started as children. What starts out as a choice quickly turns into an addiction. Tobacco is simply the delivery system for nicotine which is the active drug in tobacco. Nicotine is the number one addictive drug in use today (USDHHS, 2004).

To summarize the implications of tobacco use consider the following from the 2004 Surgeon General's report on the health consequences of smoking:

> Forty years after the first Surgeon General's report in 1964, the list of diseases and other adverse effects caused by smoking

continues to expand. Epidemiological studies are providing a comprehensive assessment of the risks faced by smokers who continue to smoke across their life spans. Laboratory research now reveals how smoking causes disease at the molecular and cellular levels. Fortunately for former smokers, studies show that the substantial risks of smoking can be reduced by successfully quitting at any age. The evidence reviewed in this and prior reports of the Surgeon General leads to the following major conclusions:

1. Smoking harms nearly every organ of the body, causing many diseases and reducing the health of smokers in general.

2. Quitting smoking has immediate as well as long-term benefits, reducing risks for diseases caused by smoking and improving health in general.

3. Smoking cigarettes with lower machine-measured yields of tar and nicotine provides no clear benefit to health.

4. The list of diseases caused by smoking has been expanded to include abdominal aortic aneurysm, acute myeloid leukemia, cataract, cervical cancer, kidney cancer, pancreatic cancer, pneumonia, periodontitis, and stomach cancer (USDHHS, 2004).

Add to these the fact that the adverse economic impact of tobacco use is in excess of $157 billion dollars each year. That's a cost of nearly a trillion dollars in just six years (USDHHS, 2004). Since the first Surgeon General's Report in 1964, 12 million (that's 12,000,000) people have died prematurely of causes attributable to tobacco use. Today, over 450,000 people are dying this way each year. Putting the tobacco issue in this perspective of its horrific health and economic consequences may make it seem daunting, but when we are able to look at it from the perspective of each child being given a real chance to choose a healthy life style, we can see that much can be done, and you are the ones to do it. Despite the gloomy information presented here, there is another way to look at it: Consider the current state of the battle against tobacco use as one full of opportunities to make a real difference in the lives of young people. Not just a difference today but for the whole rest of their lives. This is a difference that will have huge impact individually and, ultimately for all of society. Right now, the number of high school seniors smoking hovers around the 24 percent mark. If that can be reduced by half to 12 percent by 2010, it is estimated that 7.1 million lives will be spared the misery of a "smoker's death" (USDHHS, 2004). As the really great question has been posed before, "If not me then who, and if not now, when?"

In his foreword to the 2000 Surgeon General's report the Director of the Centers for Disease Control and Prevention, Jeffrey P. Koplan, M.D., M.P.H. wrote, "there is cause for optimism based on considerable public support for efforts to prevent children from becoming addicted to tobacco. If the recent pattern of increases in youth tobacco use can be reversed, we can make progress toward tobacco-free generations in the future" (USDHHS, 2000).

This reversal has begun, but for it to continue we must be as diligent as possible to see that those (you) who have the best opportunity to help kids avoid this addiction get fully engaged and have the very best resources with which to work.

Don't Get Hooked is such a resource. It is a collection of high-impact activities that easily fit into your busy schedule.

The book is broken into four sections each designed to create awareness and build the skills kids will need to fall back on when confronting the powerful temptations to begin or continue tobacco use. Since tobacco is simply the delivery system for nicotine, the first section is devoted to learning about nicotine, the implications of addiction, and what tobacco and tobacco use really is all about. The second section deals with the influences of media that play out in the lives of young people. The third section is dedicated to resistance and refusal skills. These are the skills that need to be continually developed and reinforced as kids move through childhood, into adolescence, and on into young adulthood. At the conclusion of each of the first three sections, you will find a Learning Summary that can be used to measure new knowledge that students have accumulated by having participated in each section's activities. The Learning Summary can also be used as a pre- and post-evaluation to compare where students' prior knowledge compared to the new things they have acquired as a consequence of the activities in which they have participated.

The final section of the book is an appendix of diseases and other adverse health effects caused by smoking. This last section is a wake up call to anyone who thinks tobacco use is cool and smart. Buying a ticket to a life of compromised health is both uncool and stupid. Just as Forrest Gump's mother taught him, "Stupid is as stupid does." If this seems harsh, it pales in comparison to what is at stake.

To further enhance the book's value, activities are designed to support many of the standards set forth by the American School Counselor Association's (ASCA) National Standards (2003, pp. 81-86). Among those areas of student development specifically addressed are the following:

Students will—

- A:A3.1 Take responsibility for their actions
- PS:A2.6 Use effective communication skills
- PS:B1.2 Understand consequences of decisions and choices
- PS:B1.8 Know when peer pressure is influencing a decision
- PS:CI.7 Apply effective problem-solving and decision-making skills to make safe and healthy choices
- PS:CI.8 Learn about the emotional and physical dangers of substance use and abuse
- PS:CI.9 Learn how to cope with peer pressure
- PS:CI.11 learn coping skills for managing life events.

In addition to incorporating these standards *Don't Get Hooked* activities are written across the curriculum with each activity creating a context for reinforcing learnings from important academic areas.

Enjoy your experience with *Don't Get Hooked* and let us know about other ways we can help you have the success you want helping young people grow and succeed.

References

U.S. Department of Health and Human Services. (2004). *The health consequences of smoking: A report of the surgeon general.* Retrieved March 11, 2005, from <http://www.cdc.gov/tobacco/sgr/sgr_2004/index.htm>

U.S. Department of Health and Human Services. (2000). *The health consequences of smoking: A report of the surgeon general.* Retrieved March 11, 2005, from <http://www.cdc.gov/tobacco/sgr/sgr_2000/index.htm>

American School Counselor Association. (2003). *The ASCA national model,* Alexandria, VA: American School Counselor Association.

All About Tobacco and Nicotine

Section One

This section gives you activities that engage students in broadening or reinforcing their knowledge of tobacco and the drug nicotine. Since many students may have already had exposure to similar information, it is important to determine where their level of understanding is so that you can tailor these activities to either presenting new information or revisiting and validating information they have already received. It is very important to note that repetition and presenting material in new ways is turning out to be a key in inoculating kids against the challenge of tobacco. These reviews and reintroductions keep knowledge alive for students. Another point is that it is now apparent that greater emphasis on short- and long-term health effects is being seen as critical in the prevention process. As kids are seeing more and more of the terrible prices people are paying because of tobacco use they are better able to understand that these consequences are not in some distant future, but that they start manifesting themselves in some ways almost immediately. This section includes engaging and fun activities that shine the light on why it's really dumb to use tobacco.

What Happens When You Smoke?

Information and Experiment

What this activity teaches:

- Smoking has negative short-term and long-term effects on the body.
- Learning the effects of smoking on the body can help us make wise decisions about smoking.

Notes:

You will need:

A large, empty soda bottle or other clear plastic bottle with a cap and with the label removed; cotton balls; a 3-inch tube approximately the same diameter as a cigarette; a small amount of modeling clay; matches; and one cigarette

Directions:

1. Gather the students together and announce that you are going to conduct an experiment that will introduce them to the effects of smoking. You will be making a "smoking machine" that shows what smoke does to the lungs.
2. Make sure that the plastic bottle is clean. Cut a hole in the cap that is large enough for the tube. Insert the tube in the hole so that one end extends into the bottle, and other end sticks out above the cap. Use the clay to seal the hole around the tube so that no gases can escape. Place several cotton balls inside the bottle and screw on the cap. Press the sides of the bottle to force out the air. Place the end of the cigarette in the protruding end of the tube and light it with a match. Pump the bottle slowly and steadily.

Notes:

3. "Smoke" the cigarette with the machine until it has burned down. Then open the bottle and show the cotton balls to the students. Ask them what the cotton looks like. Ask them: What do you think cigarette smoking does to the inside of your lungs?

4. Give this additional information about the effects of smoking: Short Term Effects: Blood vessels get smaller, increasing blood pressure and heart rate (making the heart work too hard). Less oxygen gets to the brain and other parts of the body because more carbon monoxide gets into the bloodstream. This slows and inhibits body functions necessary for performing well and maintaining the immune system. When a cigarette is smoked, the cilia in the bronchial tubes, which act as brooms to clean the air going into the lungs, stop working for 20 minutes. Nicotine reaches the organs of the body within 30 minutes of smoking a cigarette, triggering a desire for more nicotine (the beginning of addiction). Long-term effects: heart disease, lung cancer, emphysema, chronic and acute bronchitis, destruction of the cilia in the bronchial tubes, thickening of the walls of the arteries, and, increased risk of death.

Discussion:

Culminate the experiment by asking these and other questions:

— *After seeing what tobacco smoke does to the cotton balls, what do you think tobacco will do to human lungs?*
— *Were you surprised at how quickly the cotton became discolored? Do you think the effects on lungs could be that quick?*
— *After seeing this experiment, how do you feel about smoking?*

What Does Smoking Really Cost?

Math Activity

Notes:

Note: This activity should precede the activity, *What Can You Do With the Money?*

What this activity teaches:

- Smoking is an expensive addiction.
- The money saved by not smoking can be used to purchase many things.

You will need:

Paper and pencils for each group of students; chalkboard or chart paper on which to write the math puzzle

Directions:

1. Write the following on the board or chart paper: Jan and Jack are 15 year old twins. Jan has secretly started smoking. If cigarettes cost $3.50 a pack and Jan smokes one pack of cigarettes a day, how much will she spend on cigarettes a day, how much will she spend on cigarettes in one month? In one year? If Jan lives to be 65 years of age, how much will her cigarette habit cost her?
2. Have the students work in small groups to answer the questions.
3. Assist any groups that have trouble calculating the answers. Once all groups have answered the questions, tell the students: Jack knows about Jan's smoking and disapproves. He plans to save and invest the same amount of money that Jan spends on cigarettes. He puts his money in a bank savings

Notes:

and investment account that earns 10 percent interest. According to Jack's figures, by the time he is 65, his savings investment will amount to $1,882,424.00!

Discussion:

Ask these and other questions to generate a discussion about the disadvantages of smoking:

— *Who do you think is the wisest person, Jan or Jack? For what reasons?*
— *From an economic point of view, does smoking make sense?*
— *What would you do with all the money that Jan spent on cigarettes?*
— *What would it cost Jan to smoke two packs of cigarettes each day?*

What Can You Do With the Money?

Cooperative Activity

Notes:

Note: This activity should be preceded by the math activity, *What Does Smoking Really Cost?*

What this activity teaches:

- When we choose not to smoke, we have much more money to spend on other things.

You will need:

Catalogs of all types; chart paper, scissors, glue, writing paper, and pencils for each group

Directions:

1. Remind the students about the money they discovered can be saved by not smoking (from the previous activity, *What Does Smoking Really Cost?*).
2. Have the students work in small groups. Tell the groups to pretend that they each have the amount of money spent by Jan in one year on cigarettes ($1,277.50) and can spend it on anything they wish from the catalogs.
3. Explain that each group must work as a team, and every member of the team is to contribute at least one item. The teams should try to spend as close to $1,277.50 as possible, without going over that amount.
4. Give each group a sheet of chart paper. Have the students go through the catalogs and select the items they want. Tell them to cut out the items and paste them on the chart paper

Notes:

while keeping a running tally of the amount they are spending on a separate sheet of paper.

5. Have each group share with the class the total amount of money it spent, and describe some of the items it "purchased."

Discussion:

After the students have shared with the class, generate a discussion by asking these or other appropriate questions:

— *How long would you have to work to earn $1277.50?*
— *When people spend this amount of money on cigarettes, what do they have to show for it?*
— *What's the best way to avoid developing an expensive tobacco habit?*

How Tobacco Affects the Body

Leader Presentation and Discussion

Notes:

What this activity teaches:

- We can become acquainted with the specific harmful effects of tobacco use.
- By knowing these effects, we can make the informed choice not to use tobacco in any form.

You will need:

A copy of the experience sheet, *How Our Breathing Works*, for each student

Directions:

Read (or paraphrase) the following information to the class. Elaborate on or modify the content, descriptions, and language to best meet the comprehension levels of your students. Encourage questions and/or discussion concerning each item. You may obtain more information about tobacco and its effects from the Centers for Disease Control and Prevention at their web site <www.cdc.gov> (search under tobacco), and Campaign for Tobacco-Free Kids <http://tobaccofreekids.org>.

1. Tobacco is a plant the leaves of which are smoked in **cigarettes, cigars** and **pipes**. Tobacco is also **chewed** or **dipped** in the form of chewing or spit tobacco. Dipping tobacco is done by putting the tobacco into the mouth and letting it sit next to the gums.

2. There are many harmful substances in tobacco. The **carbon monoxide** in tobacco smoke prevents oxygen from reaching the cells in all parts of the body. When the body doesn't have enough oxygen, the smoker feels tired and lacks stamina.

Notes:

The ability to think and to perform well mentally is also diminished. When the heart receives carbon monoxide from smoke and doesn't get enough oxygen, heart disease and heart attacks may result. The body's immune system is also compromised.

3. **Nicotine** is another harmful substance in tobacco. Nicotine is a **stimulant**. Stimulants speed up the work of the body. As a stimulant, nicotine causes increased nervousness in many smokers. Nicotine also constricts blood vessels so that the circulation of blood throughout the body is impaired. Finally, nicotine is powerfully **addictive**.

4. **Tar** is also found in tobacco smoke. Tar is a dark brown sticky substance that coats the lungs of smokers and makes breathing difficult. Tar from tobacco may cause cancer cells to grow in the lungs.

5. In addition to Carbon Dioxide, Nicotine, and Tar, several **harmful gases** have been identified in tobacco smoke: Nitrogen Dioxide, Hydrogen Cyanide (the same gas used to execute criminals in the gas chamber), hydrogen sulfide, and arsenic.

6. Smoke-filled air contains visible smoke particles and gases that irritate the eyes and nasal passages of both smokers and nonsmokers.

7. Smokers are more likely than nonsmokers to get these diseases: emphysema and chronic bronchitis. Emphysema is an incurable lung disease in which the air sacks of the lungs are weakened and destroyed. People with emphysema have a hard time breathing and tire easily. Chronic bronchitis is caused by tar settling in the bronchial tubes and air passageways. Smokers with chronic bronchitis cough frequently and have a hard time breathing.

8. Smoking ten cigarettes in a closed automobile produces enough carbon monoxide to interfere with the driver's ability to judge time intervals, and can lead to accidents.

Notes:

9. When nonsmokers are exposed to tobacco smoke, these same harmful substances and gases enter their lungs. Breathing someone else's smoke can cause headache, sore throat, stuffy nose, and eye irritation. Nonsmokers exposed to tobacco smoke have a highly increased likelihood of developing the same diseases as smokers. Second hand smoke presents the same risks to nonsmokers that smokers experience.

Note: To supplement the information in items 10. and 11. it is suggested that the appendix be used to illustrate how far reaching tobacco's adverse health consequences really are.

10. Cancers of all kinds are very serious diseases in which cells grow very quickly and no longer function as they should. A smoker is much more likely than a nonsmoker to get cancer. It was once thought that only lung cancer was connected to smoking, but now not only are there many other cancers associated with smoking, but the causes of virtually every disease can be traced to tobacco use in all its forms. If not caused by tobacco virtually all diseases are made worse.

11. Beyond disease, tobacco use is now known to contribute to reproductive problems, complications with pregnancy, low birth weight and babies being delivered stillborn. Weakened bones and diminished general health are also attributable to tobacco use.

Upon completion of the presentation and discussion, give a copy of the an experience sheet, *How Our Breathing Works*, to each student. Ask volunteers to read aloud the information concerning the functioning of the lungs. As a class, try the breathing exercise. Then, have the students work independently to complete the experience sheet. To culminate the activity have the students share what they wrote on their experience sheets.

How Our Breathing Works

When you breathe in:

1. Your chest expands and your lungs fill with oxygen.
2. Blood cells inside your lungs absorb the oxygen.
3. Blood from the lungs goes to your heart.
4. Your heart pumps the blood throughout your body.
5. The oxygen in your blood cells help to keep your body healthy.

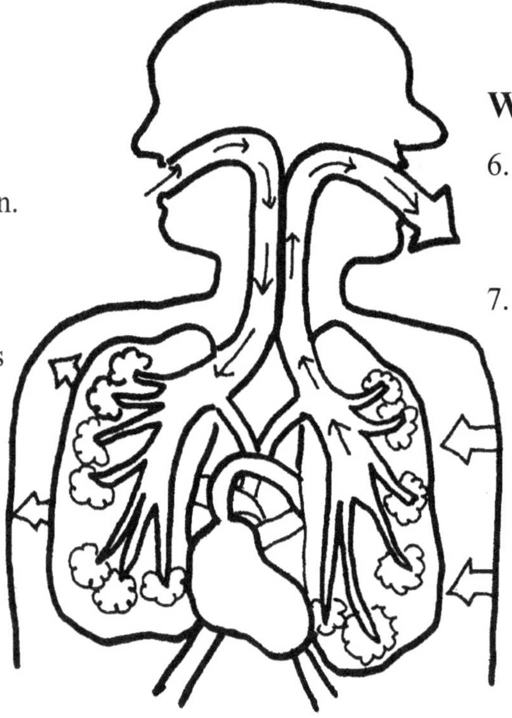

When you breathe out:

6. Your blood cells carry away carbon dioxide (CO2) from all parts of your body.
7. Your blood returns to your heart and your heart pumps it back to your lungs.
8. Your blood cells return the carbon dioxide to air inside your lungs.
9. Your chest is squeezed smaller and the air that is full of carbon dioxide is squeezed out.
10. If you smoke, you also breathe in tar and chemicals that can't be squeezed out with the air. They stay in your lungs and can cause cells to change. Some of these changed cells may become cancer.

Try this breathing exercise:

Place both hands on your rib cage, take a deep breath, and feel your lungs expand as they take in air. Now exhale and feel the lungs get smaller again. Try it several times, and then answer the following questions:

How does it feel to be able to breathe deeply and feel your lungs fill with fresh air?

____

____

Imagine what it would feel like if you smoked. Your lungs would be full of tar and you couldn't take a deep breath. Write down how you think that would feel:

____

____

List some reasons why you think it's smart never to start smoking or use tobacco in any form:

____

____

Don't Find Yourself in This Number

Geography and Math Activity

What this activity teaches:

- Puts the number of premature tobacco caused deaths into perspective.
- That the number of tobacco caused deaths is more than just a number but that it is real people who have been killed by the effects of tobacco.
- There are still huge numbers of people dying each day and each year.

You will need:

World map or globe, map of the United States that shows major cities, writing materials, a copy of the reproducible experience sheet, *Population Fact Sheets,* for each individual or small group; recent population figures for the community in which you are working

Directions:

1. Have students work as individuals or in groups of three or four.
2. Pass out a set of Population Fact Sheets to each individual or group and explain that they contain lists that rank the 227 countries of the world, the 50 United States, and the 32 largest American cities from largest to smallest.
3. Explain to the students that over the last 40 years more than 13 million people in the United States have died prematurely (before they should have) because of tobacco use, and that today, over 450,000 Americans are dying each year because of tobacco use.

Notes:

Notes:

4. Ask students to work alone or in their small groups to determine answers to the following question:

— *How many countries have populations of less than 13 million people? (answer: 162)*
— *How many states have populations of less than 13 million People? (answer: 46)*
— *How many cities in the U.S. have populations of over 13 million people (answer: 0)*

5. When the students have all arrived at their answers, make sure that their answers are correct, and explain that more people have died in the last 40 years because of tobacco use than are alive today in all those countries, states, and in every one of the largest cities in the United States.

6. Now ask the students to look at their Population Fact Sheets and answer the following questions:

— *Starting with the smallest country, how many countries' populations do you have to add together before you get to 13 million people? (answer: 67)*
— *Starting with the smallest state, how many states do you have to add together before you get to 13 million people? (answer: 13)*
— *Starting with the smallest of the 32 largest cities in the U.S., how many cities' populations do you have to add together before you reach 13 million people? (answer: 21)*

7. Ask the students to imagine what it would be like of all the people who now live in all those countries, states, and cities suddenly died. Now ask the following questions:

— *What do you think would be the world reaction to such a huge loss of life?*
— *With that many people actually having died because of tobacco use what is your reaction?*

8. Ask the students to find the countries they have identified on the world map or globe, and then ask them to find the states and cities they identified on the map of the United States.

9. Point out that the number of people who have died and will die prematurely is huge and then ask the students if they want to be in that number.

10. Knowing the population of the community in which you are working, ask the students what it would be like if this year 450,000 people died in their community. Explain that this is how many people will have their lives end in the U.S. this year because of tobacco use.

Notes:

Population Fact Sheets

The Countries of the World Ranked from Largest to Smallest

(As of April 4, 2005)

Country	Population
1 China	1,306,313,812
2 India	1,080,264,388
3 United States	295,734,134
4 Indonesia	241,973,879
5 Brazil	186,112,794
6 Pakistan	162,419,946
7 Bangladesh	144,319,628
8 Russia	143,420,309
9 Nigeria	128,765,768
10 Japan	127,417,244
11 Mexico	106,202,903
12 Philippines	87,857,473
13 Vietnam	83,535,576
14 Germany	82,431,390
15 Egypt	77,505,756
16 Ethiopia	73,053,286
17 Turkey	69,660,559
18 Iran	68,017,860
19 Thailand	64,185,502
20 Congo (Kinshasa)	60,764,490
21 France	60,656,178
22 United Kingdom	60,441,457
23 Italy	58,103,033
24 Korea, South	48,640,671
25 Ukraine	46,996,765
26 Burma	46,996,558
27 South Africa	44,344,136
28 Colombia	42,954,279
29 Spain	40,341,462
30 Sudan	40,187,486
31 Argentina	39,537,943
32 Poland	38,557,984
33 Tanzania	36,766,356
34 Kenya	33,829,590
35 Canada	32,805,041
36 Morocco	32,725,847
37 Algeria	32,531,853
38 Afghanistan	29,928,987
39 Peru	27,925,628
40 Nepal	27,676,547
41 Uganda	27,269,482
42 Uzbekistan	26,851,195
43 Saudi Arabia	26,417,599
44 Iraq	26,074,906
45 Venezuela	25,375,281
46 Malaysia	23,953,136
47 Korea, North	22,912,177
48 Taiwan	22,894,384
49 Romania	22,329,977
50 Ghana	21,946,247
51 Yemen	20,727,063
52 Australia	20,090,437
53 Sri Lanka	20,064,776
54 Mozambique	19,406,703
55 Syria	18,448,752
56 Madagascar	18,040,341
57 Cote d'Ivoire	17,298,040
58 Cameroon	16,988,132
59 Netherlands	16,407,491
60 Chile	15,980,912
61 Kazakhstan	15,185,844
62 Cambodia	13,636,398
63 Burkina Faso	13,491,736
64 Ecuador	13,363,593
65 Malawi	12,707,464
66 Niger	12,162,856
67 Zimbabwe	12,160,782
68 Guatemala	12,013,907
69 Angola	11,827,315
70 Senegal	11,706,498

71 Mali	11,415,261
72 Cuba	11,346,670
73 Zambia	11,261,795
74 Serbia and Montenegro	10,829,175
75 Greece	10,668,354
76 Portugal	10,566,212
77 Belgium	10,364,388
78 Belarus	10,300,483
79 Czech Republic	10,241,138
80 Tunisia	10,074,951
81 Hungary	10,006,835
82 Chad	9,657,069
83 Guinea	9,452,670
84 Dominican Republic	9,049,595
85 Sweden	9,001,774
86 Bolivia	8,857,870
87 Somalia	8,591,629
88 Rwanda	8,440,820
89 Austria	8,184,691
90 Haiti	8,121,622
91 Azerbaijan	7,911,974
92 Burundi	7,795,426
93 Benin	7,649,360
94 Switzerland	7,489,370
95 Bulgaria	7,450,349
96 Honduras	7,167,902
97 Tajikistan	7,163,506
98 Hong Kong S.A.R.	6,898,686
99 El Salvador	6,704,932
100 Paraguay	6,347,884
101 Israel	6,276,883
102 Laos	6,217,141
103 Sierra Leone	5,867,426
104 Libya	5,765,563
105 Jordan	5,759,732
106 Papua New Guinea	5,545,268
107 Nicaragua	5,465,100
108 Denmark	5,432,335
109 Slovakia	5,431,363
110 Togo	5,399,991
111 Finland	5,223,442
112 Kyrgyzstan	5,146,281
113 Turkmenistan	4,952,081
114 Georgia	4,677,401
115 Eritrea	4,669,638
116 Norway	4,593,041
117 Croatia	4,495,904
118 Moldova	4,455,421
119 Bosnia and Herzegovina	4,430,494
120 Singapore	4,425,720
121 Central African Republic	4,237,703
122 New Zealand	4,035,461
123 Costa Rica	4,016,173
124 Ireland	4,015,676
125 Puerto Rico	3,911,299
126 Lebanon	3,826,018
127 Congo (Brazzaville)	3,602,269
128 Lithuania	3,596,617
129 Albania	3,563,112
130 Uruguay	3,415,920
131 Panama	3,140,232
132 Mauritania	3,086,859
133 Oman	3,001,583
134 Armenia	2,982,904
135 Liberia	2,900,269
136 Mongolia	2,791,272
137 Jamaica	2,735,520
138 United Arab Emirates	2,563,212
139 West Bank	2,385,615
140 Kuwait	2,335,648
141 Latvia	2,290,237
142 Bhutan	2,232,291
143 Macedonia	2,045,262
144 Lesotho	2,031,348
145 Namibia	2,030,692
146 Slovenia	2,011,070
147 Botswana	1,640,115
148 Gambia, The	1,595,086
149 Guinea-Bissau	1,413,446
150 Gabon	1,394,307
151 Gaza Strip	1,376,289
152 Estonia	1,332,893
153 Mauritius	1,230,602
154 Swaziland	1,138,227

155 Trinidad and Tobago	1,075,066
156 East Timor	1,040,880
157 Fiji	893,354
158 Qatar	863,051
159 Cyprus	780,133
160 Reunion	776,948
161 Guyana	765,283
162 Bahrain	688,345
163 Comoros	671,247
164 Solomon Islands	538,032
165 Equatorial Guinea	529,034
166 Djibouti	476,703
167 Luxembourg	468,571
168 Macau S.A.R.	449,198
169 Guadeloupe	448,713
170 Suriname	438,144
171 Martinique	432,900
172 Cape Verde	418,224
173 Malta	398,534
174 Brunei	372,361
175 Maldives	349,106
176 Bahamas, The	301,790
177 Iceland	296,737
178 Belize	281,084
179 Barbados	278,870
180 Western Sahara	273,008
181 French Polynesia	270,485
182 Netherlands Antilles	219,958
183 New Caledonia	216,494
184 Vanuatu	205,754
185 French Guiana	195,506
186 Mayotte	193,633
187 Sao Tome and Principe	187,410
188 Samoa	177,287
189 Guam	168,564
190 Saint Lucia	166,312
191 Saint Vincent/Grenadines	117,534
192 Tonga	112,422
193 Virgin Islands	108,708
194 Micronesia	108,105
195 Kiribati	103,092
196 Jersey	90,812
197 Grenada	89,502
198 Seychelles	81,188
199 Northern Mariana Islands	80,362
200 Man, Isle of	75,049
201 Aruba	71,566
202 Andorra	70,549
203 Dominica	69,029
204 Antigua and Barbuda	68,722
205 Bermuda	65,365
206 Guernsey	65,228
207 Marshall Islands	59,071
208 American Samoa	57,881
209 Greenland	56,375
210 Faroe Islands	46,962
211 Cayman Islands	44,270
212 Saint Kitts and Nevis	38,958
213 Liechtenstein	33,717
214 Monaco	32,409
215 San Marino	28,880
216 Gibraltar	27,884
217 Virgin Islands, British	22,643
218 Cook Islands	21,388
219 Turks and Caicos Islands	20,556
220 Palau	20,303
221 Wallis and Futuna	16,025
222 Anguilla	13,254
223 Nauru	13,048
224 Tuvalu	11,636
225 Montserrat	9,341
226 Saint Helena	7,460
227 Saint Pierre and Miquelon	7,012

Source: International Database <http://www.census.gov/cgi-bin/ipc/idbrank.pl>, May 5, 2005

Population of the 50 United States from Largest to Smallest

(As of July 1, 2008)

1	California	36,756,666	18	Missouri	5,911,605	35	Nevada	2,600,167
2	Texas	24,326,974	19	Maryland	5,633,597	36	New Mexico	1,984,356
3	New York	19,490,297	20	Wisconsin	5,627,967	37	West Virginia	1,814,468
4	Florida	18,328,340	21	Minnesota	5,220,393	38	Nebraska	1,783,432
5	Illinois	12,901,563	22	Colorado	4,861,515	39	Idaho	1,523,816
6	Pennsylvania	12,448,279	23	Alabama	4,627,851	40	Maine	1,316,456
7	Ohio	11,485,910	24	South Carolina	4,479,800	41	New Hampshire	1,315,809
8	Michigan	10,003,422	25	Louisiana	4,410,796	42	Hawaii	1,288,198
9	Georgia	9,685,744	26	Kentucky	4,269,245	43	Rhode Island	1,050,788
10	North Carolina	9,222,414	27	Oregon	3,790,060	44	Montana	967,440
11	New Jersey	8,682,661	28	Oklahoma	3,642,361	45	Delaware	873,092
12	Virginia	7,769,089	29	Connecticut	3,501,252	46	South Dakota	804,194
13	Massachusetts	6,497,967	30	Iowa	3,002,555	47	Alaska	686,293
14	Washington	6,549,224	31	Mississippi	2,938,618	48	North Dakota	641,481
15	Arizona	6,500,180	32	Kansas	2,802,134	49	Vermont	621,270
16	Indiana	6,376,792	33	Arkansas	2,855,390	50	Wyoming	532,668
17	Tennessee	6,214,888	34	Utah	2,736,424			

Source: Infoplease <http://www.infoplease.com/ipa/A0004986.html>, July 1, 2008

Population of the 32 Largest American Cities from Largest to Smallest

(As of July 1, 2007)

1	New York NY	8,274,527	12	Jacksonville FL	805,605	23	Boston MA	599,351
2	Los Angeles CA	3,834,340	13	Indianapolis IN	795,458	24	Seattle WA	594,210
3	Chicago IL	2,836,658	14	San Francisco CA	764,976	25	Nashville TN	590,807
4	Houston TX	2,208,180	15	Columbus OH	747,755	26	Denver CO	588,349
5.	Phoenix AZ	1,552,259	16	Austin TX	743,074	27	Washington DC	588,292
6	Philadelphia PA	1,449,634	17	Fort Worth TX	681,818	28	Las Vegas NV	558,880
7	San Antonio TX	1,328,984	18	Memphis TN	674,028	29	Louisville KY	557,789
8	San Diego CA	1,266,731	19	Charlotte NC	671,588	30	Portland OR	550,396
9	Dallas TX	1,240,499	20	Baltimore MD	637,455	31	Oklahoma City OK	547,274
10	San Jose CA	939,899	21	El Paso TX	606,913	32	Tucson AZ	525,529
11	Detroit MI	916,952	22	Milwaukee WI	602,191			

Source: Infoplease <http://www.infoplease.com/ipa/A0763098.html>, July 1, 2007

Smoking Is a Drag!

Informative Activity and Board Game

Notes:

D	R	A	G

What this activity teaches:

- Smoking has serious negative health consequences.
- Smoking, rather than being cool, is a sign of addiction and horrible health choices.

You will need:

Pencils, writing paper, rulers, one 12-inch by 18-inch white construction paper per student, sixteen 3-inch squares of paper per student to be used as markers; overhead transparencies with colored pens and overhead projector (or large sheets of butcher paper and magic markers)

Directions:

1. **Prepare the game boards.** Distribute one piece of white construction paper to each student and demonstrate the board-construction process while the students follow along. Holding the paper vertically, measure 3 inches from the top with a ruler and mark with a pencil. Fold the paper along that 3-inch line and leave it folded. Next, make a grid of 16 rectangles by folding the remainder of the paper vertically in half and in half again; then horizontally in half and in half again. Then, unfold the paper and trace over the fold lines with a pencil or marker. Finally, unfold the reserved 3-inch border and print the word DRAG in large capital letters across the top so that each letter is directly above a column of rectangles. Explain that the students will write smoking facts inside the 16 rectangles to create a game board similar to a BINGO board.

2. **Present and discuss the facts.** Tell the students that you will be presenting some facts on the hazards of smoking, and they will need to write these facts on their game board.

Notes:

Explain: *You may write only one fact per rectangle; however, you may write it in any rectangle you choose. Scramble the facts around so that every game board is different.*

If you are using an overhead projector, write the following facts on a blank overhead transparency as you are presenting and discussing them. If you are not using an overhead, write them on butcher paper:

- The smoke from tobacco has three dangerous poisons in it: nicotine, tar, and carbon monoxide.
- Nicotine is an addictive substance in smoke. It reaches the brain within seconds of taking a drag from a cigarette. It then travels to other parts of the body in 20 to 30 minutes, creating a physiological need for another cigarette.
- Tar is a dark, sticky substance that sticks to the inside of your lungs, making it harder to breathe. It can stain your lungs brown and can also cause cancer.
- Carbon monoxide pushes the oxygen out of your cells, making it harder for them to work.
- The poisons in smoke damage the cilia in your bronchial tubes. The cilia are little hairs that sweep away the dirt so that the lungs can breath clean air.
- When the cilia are damaged, the smoker starts coughing. This is called "smoker's cough". Over a long period of time, smoker's cough can develop into a disease called chronic bronchitis.
- Smoking can cause a disease of the lungs called emphysema. It is a disease in which the air sacs in the lungs burst and the capillaries carrying oxygen from the lungs to other parts of the body are destroyed. Many people with emphysema need to carry an oxygen tank with them because their lungs don't work properly.
- Smoking can cause lung cancer. Cancer is uncontrolled and irregular growth in the lungs. Symptoms of lung cancer are coughing, blood in the mucus, chest pains, and difficulty

Notes:

breathing. Smokers are 10 times more likely to develop lung cancer than non-smokers.

- There are more deaths among cigarette smokers than among non-smokers at every age. The American Cancer Society says that men who smoke 1/2 pack of cigarettes per day have a death rate 60% higher than non-smokers. If they smoke a pack a day, the death rate is 90% higher, and two packs daily raises the rate to 120% higher.
- Smoking has been shown to cause high blood pressure, stroke, and heart attacks. Smoking causes the blood vessels to become smaller, therefore increasing blood pressure and heart rate. Smoking makes the heart work harder than it should all the time. Because blood isn't carried through the body very well, the smoker may have a lower body temperature.
- Smoking creates two kinds of smoke: mainstream smoke and second-hand or sidestream smoke. Mainstream smoke is inhaled by the smoker. Second-hand smoke is inhaled by the non-smoker and is far more dangerous. Students who live in households where someone smokes have higher rates of respiratory diseases such as bronchitis and pneumonia.
- Every pack of cigarettes must have a warning printed on it that says, "Warning: the Surgeon General Has Determined That Cigarette Smoking is Dangerous To Your Health." It has been proven that smoking does cause cancer and heart disease.
- Smoking causes fires of all kinds. Cigarette smoking causes 19% of all fires. That's 19 in every 100. Forty percent of the fires in which one or more people are killed are caused by cigarettes.
- Smoking creates bad breath, smokey-smelling clothes, and discolored teeth, as well as premature aging and wrinkles. Smoking is not glamorous or cool like advertisements show it to be.
- Smoking is addictive. An addicted person depends upon smoking and must continue smoking. Smoking usually

Notes:

becomes a habit first. Then, as a person continues to smoke, he or she becomes addicted and needs to have tobacco. Nicotine is the chemical in tobacco that causes addiction.

- Smoking causes a person's sense of taste and smell to decrease. When the sense of taste is lessened, a person may need to increase the salt and sugar in his or her food. Too much salt and sugar can also be unhealthy.

3. **Play the game.** When you have finished discussing the information above, use the game boards and markers to reinforce what the students have learned. Read one fact at a time from your list. Students who have the fact written on their DRAG game board should cover it with a marker, as they would in a BINGO game. The winner(s) is the first person to have a vertical, horizontal, or diagonal line of 4 covered facts. That person calls out, "Drag!" which ends the game. Play as many games as time allows.

Variation:

Supply groups of 5 to 8 with a list of all the facts. Instruct them to cut apart the list and place the facts in a box. Have them choose a "caller" to draw one fact at a time from the box, while they play the game as a group.

Discussion:

Conclude the activity by asking these and other questions:

— *Why is it important for us to remember facts about smoking and other tobacco use?*
— *How can knowing the facts about the bad effects of smoking help us to keep from using tobacco in the future?*
— *Why do many people avoid being around smokers?*

Chew and Spit: Smokeless Tobacco and Its Effects

Informative Activity

Notes:

What this activity teaches:

- Use of smokeless tobacco has serious and dangerous health consequences
- Smokeless tobacco carries the same kinds of health risks and addictive qualities as smoking.

You will need:

Pencils and paper, any available posters and illustrated brochures on the hazards of using snuff and chewing tobacco (Several posters and brochures are available to teachers from the American Cancer Society. Contact your local chapter to obtain a catalog of teaching materials and instructions on how to order them.)

Directions:

1. Explain to the students that you are going to play a true/false game to learn how much they already know about smokeless tobacco. Tell them that they will not be graded on their answers, and that they should indicate the answer that they think is right, even if they don't know for sure. Agree on a visual signal such as thumbs-up (true) and thumbs-down (false), or ask the students to write their answers on paper.

2. Below are nine sample statements followed by brief explanations. After asking each statement and obtaining a response from the students, elaborate on the correct response. Use the information provided, and any additional information, posters, or pictures you may have.

Notes:

- **Chewing tobacco is safe because big league baseball players use it. (False)**

  Chewing tobacco can produce harmful effects to the mouth. Frequent use and direct contact with the gums can cause white, leathery patches to form inside the mouth. These patches are called leukoplakia.

- **Chewing tobacco and snuff are both forms of smokeless tobacco. (True)**

  Chewing tobacco is shredded tobacco leaf, which the user places between the cheek and teeth. Each use consists of a golf ball-sized wad. Snuff is powdered tobacco leaf, which the user places between the bottom lip and the front teeth.

- **Snuff and chewing tobacco produce no bad effects if used for only a short period of time. (False)**

  Users spit frequently because the act of chewing increases the amount of saliva in the mouth, and the tobacco is generally not swallowed. Spitting is unsanitary. The tobacco also causes bad breath, discolored teeth, wear on tooth enamel, and tooth decay.

- **You cannot die from using smokeless tobacco like you can from smoking. (False)**

  Smokeless tobacco is carcinogenic just like smoking tobacco. That means that it can lead to cancer. Six percent of the people with oral leukoplakia develop cancer in the mouth. Research has shown that 87% of oral cancer cases result from smokeless tobacco and cigarette use. Users are also four times more likely to get mouth and throat cancer.

- **Smokeless tobacco users experience a decrease in their sense of taste and smell. (True)**

  This results in a need to use more salt and sugar in foods, which is unhealthy and can cause other problems, like diabetes and high blood pressure.

Notes:

- **Dipping snuff and chewing tobacco are cool things to do. (False)**

  They won't make you a better athlete. They discolor your teeth and give you bad breath. Is that cool?

- **You can't get addicted to smokeless tobacco like you can get addicted to cigarettes, cigars, and pipes. (False)**

  Smokeless tobacco contains nicotine, the same substance that makes you addicted to smoking tobacco. At first the nicotine may give you a feeling of well being. Later, you feel let down. This high-low effect causes you to want more and more nicotine. Nicotine also makes your blood vessels work harder to get the oxygen required by your body.

- **"Chew" is another word for smokeless tobacco. (True)**

  People use the term to make chewing tobacco sound up-beat and stylish.

- **There are no warnings on smokeless tobacco products like there are on cigarette packages. (False)**

  In 1987, a law was passed requiring one of three warnings to be printed on smokeless tobacco products. The three warnings are:

  — This product may cause gum disease and tooth loss.
  — This product is not a safe alternative to cigarettes.
  — This product may cause mouth cancer.

3. After the game, have your students share what they have learned. Ask the students to think of one new fact that they learned about the use of smokeless tobacco. Have them share their learning first with a partner, then with a group of 4 students (each pair joining another pair), and finally with a group of 8 (two foursomes combining). Let the students know that it's OK if more than one person shares the same fact. On the following day, play the true/false game again. This time, invite the students to elaborate on the answer to each question. This will help reinforce their learnings.

How Does Your Body Fare?

A Cooperative Group Project

Notes:

Note: This activity should follow the informative activities on smoking and smokeless tobacco and precede the following experience sheet, *Smokeout Crossword.*

What this activity teaches

- Many parts of the body are seriously affected by smoking and the use of smokeless tobacco products.
- Particular kinds of damage accrues to each body part.

You will need:

Six-foot lengths of white butcher paper (1 length per group of 8 to 10 students), pencils, colored markers, 4-inch by 6-inch cards (approximately 15 to 20 per group), glue, yarn

Directions:

1. Divide the students into small groups. Explain that, through art and writing, they will cooperatively demonstrate the negative effects of smoking and smokeless tobacco on the body. Ask the students to remember what they learned about smoking from the presentation on how tobacco affects the body, the "DRAG" game, and the True/False smokeless tobacco and its effects game. Have each group brainstorm a list itemizing the damage that tobacco can do to the body. When the groups have agreed on a list of a dozen or more effects (obtaining teacher help or approval, as needed), ask them to write one statement on each 5 X 8 card, using markers and large lettering.
2. Distribute the butcher paper, pencils, markers, and cards. Using pencils, ask the groups to trace the body of one student onto butcher paper. Tell them to make sure that the head is in

Notes:

profile, showing the shape of the nose and mouth. Ask them to draw in the mouth, throat, lungs, heart, etc., labeling each part. Next, ask the students to go over the lines with colored markers. Finally, have them glue their 4 X 6 cards in the spaces around the traced body, connecting each card to the appropriate body part with a piece of yarn or a marker line. Display the charts on walls or bulletin boards around the room.

3. Let each group share its drawing/diagram. Ask the students in the group to take turns reading a statement and pointing to the body part affected.

Discussion:

Conclude the activity by asking the following questions:

— *Why is it important to know how tobacco effects your body?*
— *Do you think as many people would begin , or continue to smoke or use tobacco if they knew the true facts about smoking?*
— *When you know the truth about tobacco use and what happens to your body, how does it help you make wise decisions?*
— *What is the best way to avoid becoming hooked on tobacco?*

Smokeout Crossword

Experience Sheet

Note: This is the last of six activities having to do with the hazards of smoking and other tobacco use. It should be done as a final reinforcement, following the other five.

What this activity teaches:

- There are identifiable damaging health consequences associated with the use of tobacco products.

You will need:

A copy of the experience sheet, *Smokeout Crossword* (two pages) for each student

Directions:

1. Make copies of the *Smokeout Crossword*, and distribute them to your students as homework.
2. Explain that this is an opportunity for the students to do homework with a parent or adult caregiver. Their task is to complete the crossword puzzle cooperatively with the adult and in the process explain the information they have learned from the previous activities. This gives the students the opportunity to share what they know and might provide the adult with some new information as well.
3. Ask the students to return their completed crossword puzzles and review their answers with them using the answer key.

Notes:

ANSWER KEY:

ACROSS:

4. patches
5. tar
7. oxygen
8. cancer
10. smaller
11. sidestream
13. bronchitis
14. destroyed
15. deaths
17. pressure
19. chew
20. tobacco

DOWN:

1. breath
2. warnings
3. taste
6. poisons
9. nicotine
12. mainstream
16. teeth
18. cough

Smokeout Crossword

ACROSS:

4. Leukoplakia are white leathery ___________ that form inside the mouth as a result of using smokeless tobacco.
5. A dark substance that sticks to the inside of your lungs, making it difficult to breathe.
7. Carbon monoxide pushes the __________ out of your cells, making it harder for them to work.
8. An uncontrolled and irregular growth in the lungs caused by smoking.
10. Smoking causes the blood vessels to become ____________.
11. The smoke inhaled by the non-smoker when someone close is smoking.
13. When smoker's cough lasts over a long period of time, it is called __________________.
14. Emphysema is a disease in which air sacs in the lungs burst and capillaries carrying oxygen are _____________.
15. There are more ____________ among cigarette smokers than among non-smokers at any age.
17. Smoking increases the blood ___________ and heart rate.
19. Another word for smokeless tobacco.
20. Most cases of oral cancer are the result of the use of ___________ products.

DOWN:

1. Dipping snuff and chewing tobacco will make your teeth discolor and give you bad __________.
2. In 1987, a law was passed that required one of three ___________ to be placed on smokeless tobacco products.
3. Tobacco users experience a decrease in their sense of smell and __________.
6. Smoke from tobacco has three dangerous ______________ in it.
9. The substance found in all tobacco products that makes it addictive.
12. Smoke that is inhaled by the smoker.
16. Using snuff or chewing tobacco can cause excessive wear on your __________.
18. When cilia in the bronchial tubes are damaged, the smoker develops smoker's ____________.

Smokeout Crossword

As you answer the questions on the attached page, enter your answers where you see the number of the question you're answering

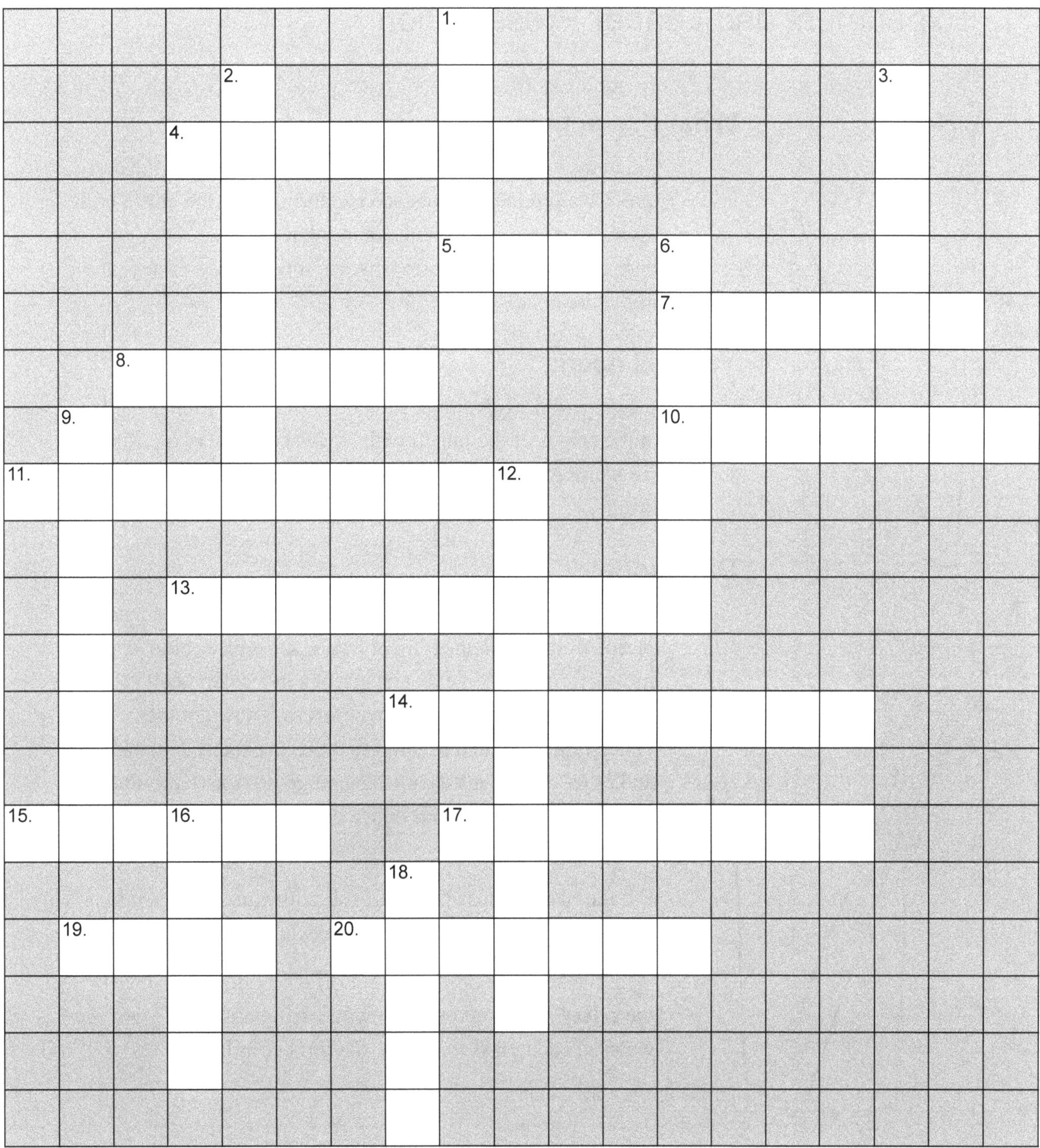

Rivers and Streams of the Body

Experiment and Leader Presentation

Notes:

What this activity teaches:

- The body's own circulatory system quickly spreads the dangerous by-products of tobacco use throughout the entire body.
- There is no safe way to engage in tobacco use.
- there is a direct connection between tobacco use, illness and premature death.

You will need:

Two celery stalks (one large stalk, and another mid-size stalk from the center of the bunch with leaves still on), two clear 12 ounce water glasses, a small paring knife, and blue food coloring

Directions:

1. Explain to the students that they will be observing an experiment that will show them how a substance (blue water) moves through the veins and arteries in a celery stalk. Explain that, as they observe this process, you want them to understand and keep in mind that this is exactly how nicotine and other dangerous chemicals and gasses move through the bloodstream and into our entire body when we engage in tobacco use.

2. Fill the two glasses about half full with water, and add several drops of the food coloring to each.

3. With the students observing cut off the bottom half-inch of the celery stalks, and place one in each glass. Gently stir the water in each glass to diffuse the food coloring.

4. Place both glasses near a window or under a bright light.
5. Tell the students that they will begin to see results in two or three hours, but it will take a full day for the final result.
6. When the time has passed, examine the celery with your students.
7. Notice how the veins of the celery have carried the coloring into the leaves and throughout the whole stalk. Cut the tip off the top of the larger stalk so that the students can see the food coloring in the veins. Explain that all plants have veins just like our bodies have veins and arteries that act like rivers and streams that carry blood to every part of our bodies. Just as the food coloring was carried throughout the celery, the harmful and dangerous products of tobacco use are carried throughout every part of our bodies.
8. Point out that it is for this reason that tobacco use threatens every part of our body with its damaging and deadly effects.
9. To further illustrate how widespread the impact of tobacco use is refer to the appendix and review with the students the cancer, cardiovascular, and respiratory diseases that result from tobacco use.

Notes:

Tell Me Your Story

Interview and Discussion Guidelines

Notes:

What this activity teaches:

- How people feel about smoking and nonsmoking.
- The negative influences that contribute to smoking.
- The positive influences that contribute to nonsmoking.

You will need:

One copy of each interview form for each student

Directions:

1. Pass out both copies of the interview forms to each student.
2. Explain that you want the students to interview two people —a smoker and a nonsmoker—who are at least 18 years old. They are to ask the questions on the forms. Review the questions with the students to make sure they understand how to proceed with the interviews.
3. Spend some time helping the students to come up with their own additional questions to list at the bottom of their interview forms.
4. Explain that the students will have three days to conduct the first interview and write down the responses of the smoker, after which they will have an opportunity to talk about some of the things they learned in class or in a group. The students will then have three more days to conduct the second interview and write down the responses of the nonsmoker. Again, they will have an opportunity to report their findings in class or their group.

5. Offer the students the following tips for conducting effective interviews:

   - Ask the first question and then stop talking. Listen carefully to the answer.
   - Look into the interviewee's eyes as he or she speaks.
   - When the interviewee stops speaking, write down his or her response.
   - Read back what you have written aloud, and ask the interviewee if you heard the answer correctly. Make changes, if necessary.
   - Ask the remaining questions in the same manner.
   - During the interview, let the interviewee know you appreciate his or her honest answers. Thank him or her when the interview ends.

Notes:

Discussion:

Conduct a discussion of the interviews with smokers. Here are several questions that will help the students recall and analyze the collective responses of the interviews with smokers:

— *About how old were most of the smokers when they started smoking?*
— *What were some of the things that influenced them to start?*
— *Why do they smoke now?*
— *How do most of them feel about their smoking?*
— *How many tried to quit and what happened when they did?*
— *What is the most important thing you learned from this interview?*

Conclude this part of the activity by acknowledging the students for their effective interviewing and reporting.

Conduct a second discussion of the interviews with nonsmokers. Here are several questions to ask the students. Allow them to answer within the context of a free-flowing discussion:

— *Some of the nonsmokers we interviewed did smoke at one time. How old were they when they first started?*

Notes:

— *What influenced most of them to be (or to become) nonsmokers?*
— *How do most of them feel about being nonsmokers?*
— *How do the nonsmokers we interviewed feel about being around people who smoke? Why do you think they have those feelings?*
— *What seem to be the biggest differences between the smokers and the non-smokers?*

6. Assist the students as they recall and analyze the collective responses of their interviewees. Note the following similarity between both groups: Some of the people who don't smoke now, did smoke at one time, and most of them probably began smoking at about the same age as the people who still smoke. Be sure they understand that most smokers don't feel good about their smoking, while nonsmokers do feel good about being smoke-free. Not only that, most nonsmokers prefer being around people who don't smoke. Focus on other key differences between the smokers and nonsmokers.

7. Conclude the activity by once again acknowledging the students for their effective interviewing and reporting.

Tell Me Your Story

Smoker Interview Form

Talk to a smoker who is at least 18 years old. Find out what happened when he or she was younger that influenced him or her to start smoking.

Here are some questions to ask the smoker (write in the answers):

1. Why do you smoke? ______________________________

____

2. How old were you when you started smoking? ______________________________

____

3. What influenced you to start? ______________________________

____

4. How do you feel about your smoking? ______________________________

____

5. Have you ever tried to quit and, if so, what happened? ______________________________

____

Think of some other questions you'd like to ask and write the questions and answers in the spaces provided below.

Question: ______________________________

Answer: ______________________________

____

Question: ______________________________

Answer: ______________________________

____

Tell Me Your Story

Nonsmoker Interview Form

Talk to a nonsmoker who is at least 18 years old. Find out what happened when he or she was younger that influenced him or her not to smoke.

Here are some questions to ask the smoker (write in the answers):

1. Did you ever smoke and, if so, how old were you when you started smoking?______

____

2. What influenced you to be (or become) a nonsmoker? ______________

____

3. How do you feel about being a nonsmoker? ______________

____

4. How do you feel about being around people who smoke? ______________

____

____

____

Think of some other questions you'd like to ask and write the questions and answers in the spaces provided below.

Question: _______________________________________

Answer: ____

____

Question: _______________________________________

Answer: ____

____

Please Don't Smoke or Chew

Discussion and Experience Sheet

What this activity teaches:

- Children and adolescents should never start using or even experimenting with tobacco products.
- There are many things that can be done to help others stay away from tobacco use.

You will need:

A copy of the experience sheet, *Please Don't Smoke or Chew*, for each student, writing materials and chart paper

Directions:

1. Divide the students into small groups. Pass out a sheet of chart paper and a large marking pen to each group.
2. Ask each group to write at the top of its chart paper the heading "Reasons Not to Smoke or Chew." Direct the groups to brainstorm all the reasons they can think of why a person shouldn't smoke or chew tobacco, and list these reasons on their chart paper.
3. When the groups have filled their chart paper, have them share what they have written with the other groups. Display the charts as a reference for the completion of the experience sheet.
4. Pass out the experience sheets to the students, and elaborate on the directions for writing a letter convincing a friend not to use tobacco. Ask the students to refer to the charts they have just finished and to put the important points they came up with into a letter format. Remind them to write a strong, convincing letter.

Notes:

Notes:

5. When all the students have completed their letters, ask for volunteers to read their letters to the other students.

Discussion:

Conclude the activity by asking these and other questions:

— *How has your letter convinced you not to use tobacco products?*
— *Why is choosing not to smoke or chew the smart choice?*
— *If your friend still wanted to use a tobacco product after your letter, what would you think of him or her?*

Please Don't Smoke or Chew

Letter to a Friend

Dear,

Your Friend,

If you had a friend who was going to start using tobacco, either smoking or chewing, what would you say that would persuade him or her not to start. In the space above write a strong and convincing letter to your friend.

What I Know About Tobacco and Nicotine

Learning Evaluation

Notes:

Note: This activity may be used before you begin this section to see where students are with their prior knowledge and then again after they have participated in the activities in this section. This pre- post evaluation is useful to gauge student progress and learning acquisition. Be sure to collect the completed Learning Summaries from the pre-evaluation so that you and the students can compare them to the post-evaluation.

What this activity teaches:

- Knowledge about tobacco and nicotine allows us to make informed decisions.
- Tobacco use is dangerous, unwise, uncool, and foolish.

You will need:

Copies of the two-page Learning Summary, *What I Know About Tobacco and Nicotine*, for each student

Directions:

1. Acknowledge the students for the work they have done in completing the activities that help them understand more about the dangerous effects of tobacco use.
2. Now that the students have completed these activities it is a good time to see what they have learned. To accomplish this you can ask them to complete the *What I Know About Tobacco and Nicotine* Learning Summary.

Notes:

3. Pass out one Learning Summary set to each student. Review the instructions for both parts of the summary with the students and make sure they understand how to proceed. Provide them enough time to complete the summary (about ten minutes).
4. After they have completed the exercise, you may gather the completed summaries for review and correction, or you may let the students self-correct their summaries.
5. Review the answers to each question with the students and answer any questions they may have. If you had the students complete the Learning Summaries before you began the activities in this section, hand out the initial evaluations and let the students see the differences in their scores.
6. Conclude the activity by again acknowledging the students for their efforts.

Answer Key:

Part I

1. True
2. True
3. False
4. True
5. True
6. True
7. False
8. False
9. False
10. True

Part II

1. oxygen
2. nicotine
3. money
4. stimulant
5. tobacco
6. tar
7. emphysema
8. dangerous
9. bad breath
10. second-hand

What I Know About Tobacco and Nicotine

Part I.

At the end of each sentence, write the word "True" if you think it is correct, or write the word "False" if you think it is incorrect.

1. When a cigarette is smoked, blood vessels get smaller, increasing blood pressure and heart rate which makes the heart work too hard. ____________
2. The cilia in the bronchial tubes of the lungs act as a broom to clean the air going into the lungs. Cigarette smoke will stop the cilia from working for 20 minutes. ____________
3. Nicotine is the only harmful substance in tobacco. ____________
4. Smokers are more likely than nonsmokers to get the diseases of emphysema and chronic bronchitis. ____________
5. Nonsmokers exposed to tobacco smoke have a highly increased likelihood of developing the same diseases as smokers. ____________
6. Smoking is an expensive habit. ____________
7. It has not been scientifically proven that smoking causes cancer and heart disease. ____________
8. Smoking is dangerous, but chewing tobacco and snuff are safe. ____________
9. Smoking only affects the lungs in a dangerous way. ____________
10. Never smoking and never using smokeless tobacco products is the best way to avoid becoming addicted. ____________

Part II.

Complete each sentence by writing the correct word from the following word list in the blank space.

(money, second-hand, stimulant, nicotine, bad breath, tobacco, tar, oxygen, emphysema, dangerous)

1. Less ____________________ gets to the brain and other parts of the body when you smoke a cigarette.
2. Within 30 minutes of smoking a cigarette ____________________ reaches the organs of the body, triggering a desire for more cigarettes.
3. You will have more ____________________ if you don't smoke cigarettes and don't use smokeless tobacco products.
4. Nicotine is a ____________________ that speeds up the work of the body and can cause increased nervousness.
5. Over 450,000 Americans die each year because of ____________________ use.
6. Smoke from tobacco contains ____________________ which is a dark, sticky substance that sticks to the inside of your lungs, making it harder to breathe.
7. Many people with ____________________, a disease often caused by smoking, need to carry an oxygen tank with them because their lungs don't work properly.
8. Every pack of cigarettes must have a warning printed on it that says, "Warning: The Surgeon General Has Determined That Cigarette Smoking is ____________________ to your health.
9. Smoking creates ____________________, smoky-smelling clothes, and discolored teeth.
10. ____________________ smoke is inhaled by nonsmokers and can be just as dangerous as mainstream smoke.

Power of Media Influence

Section Two

This section gives you information and activities that engage students in building their awareness of the efforts of the tobacco industry to get young people to smoke through its incredibly powerful advertising machine. In 1984 the tobacco industry spent $2.4 billion to promote its products. Today the industry spends over $11 billion a year to persuade those who smoke to continue, to persuade those who are beginning to keep after it, and to persuade those who have yet to start to take that first puff or dip. Where does all that money come from? It comes from the victims of tobacco addiction. Recall the amount of money a single smoker is likely to invest in the profits of the tobacco industry and you can see why it is willing to spend so much to lure young people into its addictive trap. At the same time the industry is pouring billions into this effort it is being forced to create advertising that ostensibly is designed to prevent smoking. An analysis of these adds demonstrates that their messages are weak, mostly ineffective, and at worst, designed to give the message that smoking, though dangerous, is still something that is "cool" to do. Students get a chance to see what advertising can do and how insidiously it is designed to draw them into a life of addiction and declining health.

Where's the Truth?

Leader Presentation, Discussion, and Experience Sheet

What this activity teaches:

- The tobacco industry needs new customers and will pay whatever price it takes.
- Advertising and promotion has a powerful influence in attracting new tobacco users and keeping current users hooked.
- Awareness of media impact is vital to avoiding its influence.

You will need:

Copies of the experience sheet, *Something Stinks*, for each student

Directions:

1. In your own words and at a level your students will really understand, discuss the following information. Explain to the students that the advertising messages created by the tobacco industry that promote the use of tobacco are all designed to persuade people who smoke to continue to do so, to persuade those who are just beginning to use tobacco to continue to do so, but mostly they are designed to persuade people who aren't using tobacco to start. Ask the students why the focus is on non users. After a few responses point out that the industry doesn't need to spend very much money on advertising to users because they are already addicted. Because of this, the bulk of the advertising effort is aimed at non users, and in particular, to young people.

2. Explain that tobacco companies are also required to create ads that advise young people that tobacco use is risky, but that even these ads have the effect of communicating that, while risky, tobacco use isn't such a bad thing. These ads also make the risks seem as though they are a long way off and not something to be too concerned about right now. These ads never address the economic impacts of use. They never

Notes:

Notes:

mention how much money it takes to support a tobacco habit, nor do they mention the costs associated with the diseases caused by tobacco use and the costs associated with premature death. The advertising that the tobacco industry creates to promote tobacco use also influences young people even though the law says that these ads cannot be directed specifically to young people. According to the 2004 Surgeon General's Report, tobacco ads continue to strongly influence young people by showing use "as adventurous and glamorous adult behavior." In this way tobacco use provides young people a perceived transition from studenthood to adulthood. In addition, the personal factors most often associated with smoking initiation include the young person's belief that cigarette smoking is linked with positive functions, such as having a positive social image and bonding with a peer group. Among young women, smoking may be viewed as a means of weight control (USDHHS 2004).

3. Go on to explain that young people tend to overestimate the prevalence of smoking among people their own age and among adults. Such perceptions—and in general, susceptibility to becoming a smoker—are likely to be strongly influenced by the effects of advertising. Young people who perceive high levels of smoking among their peers and who report that peers are more likely to approve of cigarette smoking are more likely to become smokers themselves (USDHHS, 2004). Ask the students to look around and they will see that far more people don't use tobacco than do, and that these people have much happier and healthier life styles. In addition, while advertising suggests that smoking may be cool, most people look at smokers as being out of control and unable to manage an addiction. Tobacco use is a smelly, unhealthy business. No really "cool" person would chose to do that. Cool people manage their lives and are not easily swayed or controlled by something like the tobacco industry.

4. An extremely important concept to communicate to the students is the fact that tobacco advertising tries very hard to

Notes:

convince young people that by using tobacco they will prove that they are "cool" and self-assured, but that in fact, just the opposite is true. Kids who start using tobacco products do so because they are very unsure of themselves. Although they think by smoking or chewing, others will think they are cool it really says loud and clear that inside they really don't feel cool, and in fact, are very unsure of themselves. Be sure to convey this point to the students.

5. Ask the students who they think really pays for the cost of advertising. Point out that for the tobacco industry to be able to spend over $11 billion dollars a year on promoting tobacco products they must make profits far in excess of that number. This profit comes from the people who use and are addicted to their products.

6. As a final part of this presentation ask students how else the tobacco industry presents tobacco use in ways that influence us. As ideas come forth, point out that we see tobacco use in movies and on television. It is also very important to point out that when other people use tobacco they inadvertently promote its use. Think of how we are influenced to try something when people around are doing it. When people around us are drinking a particular soft drink, or are wearing a particular designer brand of clothing we tend to want to join in. The same thing holds true of tobacco use. Very subtly all the people who use tobacco have become advertisements for its use by others. This is just another way tobacco users are manipulated.

7. To help students understand how much they are exposed to tobacco use in ways that are designed to get them hooked tell them that they will be doing an observation activity using the following experience sheet, *Something Stinks!*

Discussion

After providing the information above, engage students in a brief discussion using the following questions:

— *How does advertising work to influence us?*

Notes:

— *How does paying attention to tobacco advertising make us more able to avoid tobacco use?*
— *Who pays for tobacco advertising (really)?*
— *When you see kids using tobacco, what do you think of them? Do you think they are as "cool" as they do?*

8. Hand out a copy of the experience sheet, *Something Stinks!*, to each student, and tell the students that they will be using the sheets to record all the places that they see tobacco being used and how they feel about that use. This can include the people with whom they associate, people they see using tobacco in other places, and tobacco use in the media (i.e., on TV, in the movies, in magazines, etc.). Give the students a few days to complete their work and bring them back together for an additional discussion.

Discussion:

To facilitate a final discussion use the following questions:
— *How does seeing someone else smoking seem like advertising?*
— *How does seeing tobacco use in so many places surprise you?*
— *What kinds of things were not included in the tobacco use you noticed in the media? (Include things like there wasn't any smoke, nothing was mentioned about health dangers, cost of tobacco use wasn't mentioned, etc.)*
— *In what ways do you feel more in control after learning about how the tobacco industry tries to manipulate us with all its efforts to promote tobacco use?*

References

U.S. Department of Health and Human Services. (2004). *The health consequences of smoking: A report of the surgeon general*. Retrieved March 11, 2005, from <http://www.cdc.gov/tobacco/sgr/sgr_2004/index.htm>

Something Stinks!

Observation Form

Observe all the places you see tobacco being used in any form. Remember, tobacco is used in more than just cigarettes. It's also used in chewing tobacco and cigars too. Use this experience sheet to keep track of what you see and how you feel about it.

- **People around you who use tobacco (Family, friends, or others you know):**

How many people do you know who smoke or chew tobacco? ____________________

How does their tobacco use make you feel about tobacco? ____________________

____

____

...about them? ____

____

____

- **Advertising that promotes tobacco use:**

Where do you see these ads? ____

____

What do you think about these ads? ____

____

What don't tobacco ads tell us? ____

____

- **Other places I see tobacco use (Sporting events, movies, TV, on the street, etc.):**

How does tobacco use show up in these places? ____

____

How does seeing people using tobacco make you feel? ____________________

____

Advertising Tactics

Observation and Discussion

Notes:

Note: This activity should be followed by *The Real Truth* art activity.

What this activity teaches:

- The messages in advertisements can fool people into buying products.
- Understanding the tactics used by companies to sell products can help us make wise decisions about their purchase and use.

You will need:

Magazines with advertisements for tobacco products

Directions:

1. Ask the students: Have you ever seen a magazine ad for cigarettes, cigars, or smokeless tobacco? Introduce the students to some of the techniques that companies use to sell tobacco in magazine advertisements. Write the following list on the board and discuss each item with the students.

2. Advertising Tactics:

   - Wealth (the product will make you look like you are rich)
   - Escape (beautiful country scenes)
   - Bandwagon (everyone else is smoking or drinking it; be popular)
   - Romance (the product will make you more attractive to the opposite sex)
   - Glamor Girl (the product will make you beautiful)
   - Macho Man (the product will make you rugged and carefree)
   - Athletics (this is what the pros use)

3. List any other techniques that come to mind, and ask the students if they can think of more. Show and discuss examples from several magazines.
4. Distribute the magazines. Working in pairs or small groups, have the students locate at least one ad that demonstrates an advertising tactic from the list. Ask the students to show their ads to the group, explaining how the ads try to mislead the reader. Discuss the truth in relation to the false reality presented in each ad.

Notes:

Discussion:

After the groups have shared their tobacco ads and identified the misleading nature of each, ask the following questions:

— *What was the first thing to catch your attention as you looked at your ad?* (Repeat and emphasize the things the students say such as bright colors, pretty pictures, the size of the ad, attractive people, exciting activities, etc.)
— *When you find the Surgeon General's warning message in the ad, does it stand out? Is it brightly colored like the rest of the ad?*
— *Do you think the tobacco companies want the warning message to catch our attention? ...Why?*

5. As a follow up to this activity, you may want to explain that, because tobacco use is so dangerous to people and such a threat to public health, laws have been passed preventing advertising on radio and television. But the tobacco industry has been very sly in finding ways around those laws. Although it doesn't pay for regular commercials, it gets its ads on television in other ways. Ask the students where they have noticed subtle ads on TV. Help the students to recognize that when they see ads on score boards, or walls of sports arenas during sporting events, these are ways tobacco companies continue to advertise. They also put ads on racing cars and drivers protective suits and their brand names appear on athletic clothing.

Notes:

6. Ask the students to observe all the places they see cigarettes, cigars and smokeless tobacco promoted on television. Ask them to keep a list and to report back to the rest of the class what they find. Remind them to be observant and see if they can find ways in addition to those identified earlier in this activity.

7. As a last reminder, tell the students that these clever ad tactics are the ways tobacco companies try to manipulate people into beginning and continuing the use of tobacco.

The Real Truth

Art Activity

Notes:

Note: This activity should follow the *Advertising Tactics* activity.

What this activity teaches:

- Ad makers frequently try to sell us products by appealing to our emotions and fantasies.
- Many ads distort or omit the truth about the products they sell.
- Knowing the truth about how advertisements try to fool us can equip us to make better choices about alcohol and tobacco products.

You will need:

Magazine ads for tobacco products (from the previous activity), white construction paper, scissors, glue, and magic markers

Directions:

1. Divide the students into small groups and distribute the art materials to each group. Tell the students that they are going to participate in an "anti-ad campaign" to reveal the ways in which tobacco ads attempt to fool people.
2. **Explain:** *Select a magazine ad that sells a tobacco product. You may use one that we've discussed previously, or find a new one. Trim the ad neatly and glue it onto the construction paper. Next, identify the ways in which the ad tries to "hook" or mislead the reader, so that the reader will want to buy the product. Then make up short statements that reveal the truth about the product in order to "unhook " the reader. For example, if your ad shows a couple sitting in the country smoking cigarettes by a stream, you could say, "Smoking doesn't make the air cleaner, only more polluted." Or, "Notice that this picture doesn't show the SMOKE!" Write your*

Notes:

statements in bright-colored markers beside, above, or below the ad, emphasizing important words with contrasting colors.

3. Encourage the students to be creative. They may come up with some gruesome statements, but if the statements are true and appropriate, accept them. Display the "anti-ads" around the room.

Discussion:

Culminate the activity by asking these and other questions:

— *How do the pictures and words in advertisements influence people to use tobacco?*

— *Do you think that people who have been influenced by tobacco ads to smoke or use tobacco realize that they have been influenced?*

— *Do you think that people who smoke are really like the people in the smoking advertisements?*

— *Do you think that people who smoke or use tobacco let themselves be tricked into doing so?*

The Truth About Tobacco Ads

Art and Discussion Activity

Notes:

Note: This activity should follow the previous two activities on tobacco advertising and after several activities dealing with the harmful effects of tobacco use.

What this activity teaches:

- Tobacco ads aren't truthful.
- Ad makers try to make us change our minds in favor of using tobacco products.
- By knowing the real truth in tobacco ads, we are less likely to be fooled by them.

You will need:

Art materials, one copy of the experience sheet, *Truth In Advertising*, for each student

Directions:

1. Begin this activity by asking the students to share something they learned about tobacco advertising from the previous two activities.

2. Next, ask the students to share something they learned about the harmful effects of tobacco use on both smokers and chewers.

3. Pass out the art supplies and the experience sheet to the students, and explain that they are going to create their own truthful packaging for a pack of cigarettes and a container of smokeless tobacco.

4, Explain: *We all have learned that cigarettes and smokeless tobacco harm people's bodies in many serious ways. Tobacco products make people smell, and look bad. We also*

Notes:

learned that, although kids start using cigarettes and smokeless tobacco because they think it makes them look cool (like the ads suggest), it really says to everyone else that they are very unsure of themselves and easily fooled. By keeping all these things in mind, what do you think would be important to put on the cover of these packages to tell the real truth about what's inside?

5. Tell the students that they can be serious or humorous in their packaging designs, but to try to make the overall designs eye catching. Remind the students that, in addition to words and pictures, there are many other ways to communicate the truth such as the name of the brand, the logo, the colors used, where things are placed on the package, etc.
6. When the students have finished, ask them to share what they have created.

Discussion:

Culminate the activity by asking the students to remark on what they have learned about the influences of tobacco advertising.

Truth in Advertising

Create your own truthful packaging designs for the covers of a pack of cigarettes and a container of smokeless tobacco.

What I Know About Media Influence

Learning Evaluation

Notes:

Note: This activity may be used before you begin this section to see where students are with their prior knowledge and then again after they have participated in the activities in this section. This pre- post evaluation is useful to gauge student progress and learning acquisition. Be sure to collect the completed Learning Summaries from the pre-evaluation so that you and the students can compare them to the post-evaluation.

What this activity teaches:

- Media influence is broad and pervasive.
- Through careful manipulation and without knowing its power, media can persuade us to begin using tobacco products.

You will need:

Copies of the two-page Learning Summary, *What I Know About the Power of Media Influence*, for each student

Directions:

1. Acknowledge the students for the work they have done in completing the activities that help them understand the power of media influence as the tobacco industry tries to turn young people into users.

2. Now that the students have completed these activities it is a good time to see what they have learned. To accomplish this you can ask them to complete the *What I Know About the Power of Media Influence* Learning Summary.

3. Pass out one Learning Summary set to each student. Review the instructions for both parts of the summary with the students and make sure they understand how to proceed. Provide them enough time to complete the summary (about ten minutes).
4. After they have completed the exercise, you may gather the completed summaries for review and correction, or you may let the students self-correct their summaries.
5. Review the answers to each question with the students and answer any questions they may have. If you had the students complete the Learning Summaries before you began the activities in this section, hand out the initial evaluations and let the students see the differences in their scores.
6. Conclude the activity by again acknowledging the students for their efforts.

Notes:

Answer Key:

Part I	Part II
1. True	1. smokers
2. False	2. money
3. True	3. young people
4. True	4. cool
5. False	5. smelly
6. True	6. unsure
7. False	7. advertising
8. False	8. fool
9. True	9. commercials
10. True	10. manipulate

What I Know About the Power of Media Influence

Part I.

At the end of each sentence, write the word "True" if you think it is correct, or write the word "False" if you think it is incorrect.

1. One of the things that tobacco advertising is designed to do is to persuade people who aren't using tobacco to start. ____________
2. Tobacco advertising is careful to explain that using tobacco products is a very expensive habit. ____________
3. Tobacco advertising tries to influence young people by showing tobacco use as adventurous and glamorous adult behavior. ____________
4. Advertising wants people to believe that smoking may be cool, but most people look at smokers as being out of control and unable to manage an addiction. ____________
5. The tobacco industry only spends about one million dollars a year on advertising. ____________
6. Because tobacco use is so dangerous to people, laws have been passed preventing advertising on radio, television, and billboards. ____________
7. Tobacco ads on racing cars and brand names on clothing are really not a form of advertising. ____________
8. Tobacco companies design the warning labels that the Surgeon General requires to be on all cigarette packs to really stand out. ____________
9. Through their advertising, tobacco companies try to trick people into believing that tobacco use is glamorous and sexy. ____________
10. By understanding how advertising tries to trick you into believing tobacco products are something you want, you will be able to make better choices. ____________

Part II.

Complete each sentence by writing the correct word from the following word list in the blank space.

(fool, young people, smelly, money, smokers,
manipulate, unsure, commercials, cool, advertising)

1. ____________________ are the people who really pay for tobacco advertising because they continue to by tobacco products.
2. It takes a lot of ____________________ to support a tobacco habit.
3. The tobacco companies create ads promoting tobacco use that influence _____________ _____________ even though the law says that they can't.
4. One way advertising tries to mislead people is by suggesting that smoking is ____________________.
5. One thing tobacco advertising never says is that smoking is ____________________.
6. Although tobacco advertising doesn't tell you this, the main reason kids start to use tobacco products is because they are very ____________________ of themselves.
7. The yearly ____________________ budget for tobacco industry is over $12.4 Billion dollars.
8. Tobacco advertising can ____________________ people into buying its products.
9. Although the tobacco industry can't buy ____________________ it gets its ads on television in other ways.
10. Clever ad tactics are the way that tobacco companies try to ____________________ people into beginning and continuing the use of tobacco.

Refusal Skills and Taking Control

Section Three

Today, students are taught to obey their parents and teachers, and to behave in ways that are pleasing to others. Understandably, they get plenty of practice saying yes-and often develop a real inability to say no. They need to learn that sometimes a firm NO to someone else—particularly if that person is offering them something that is harmful—is a big YES to them. By practicing the skills of refusal, students will examine their abilities to say no. This section gives you activities that engage students in learning about and practicing saying no in a variety of situations so they can be better prepared for real life situations. Students must have this practice before they encounter the pressures to use tobacco. Real skill and determination are required in overcoming peer pressure and to still maintain friendships. It is important to define the skills of refusal—skills of refusal enable students to say no when they want to and to do it effectively.

Skills of refusal are important because wherever students go, they're likely to meet other kids and adults who will invite and urge them to use tobacco. So that students are able to combat inappropriate decisions three things are vital:

- They need to develop confidence
- They need to practice skills of refusal
- They need to reinforce their individuality

This section gives kids an opportunity to move forward in all three of these areas.

Time to Really Say NO!

Leader Presentation and Discussion

Notes:

Note: This activity is the first of three that work together in developing and practicing refusal skills. They should be done in sequence. In the third activity, *Practice, Practice, Practice*, students will have an opportunity to role play refusal situations where they will be able to get experience with what is presented in this activity.

What this activity teaches:

- Refusal Skills are important in all parts of our lives.
- Being able to say no generates respect for self and the respect of others.
- Saying no is the most important skill in avoiding tobacco use.

You will need:

Whiteboard or chart pad with appropriate markers

Directions:

1. Explain to the students that as they pass through life there will be things they learn that will be highly valued. As most people reflect on their lives, they almost all indicate that having Refusal Skills and being able to say "no" are among those most important learnings.
2. Continue by telling the students that these skills have more to do with life than just avoiding tobacco and drug use. These skills keep us from making commitments that we won't be able to honor. They allow us to maintain control of our lives rather than giving up control to other people and things when we "just can't say no." Perhaps the most important thing having these skills gives to us is the *feeling* that we are in control, and with that comes a growing respect for ourselves and the respect of other people who will admire

Notes:

our ability to bring control to our lives and to any situation in which we find ourselves.

3. Now explain that, in addition to saying no, we must look and sound in control to show others that we mean what we are saying. Help students understand the following:

Body language must communicate self-confidence, clear purpose, and control:

- Good posture with a straight back whether sitting, standing or walking.
- Face the peer and maintain eye contact.
- Look proud, strong, confident (even when not feeling much like it).

These things give you the *look* of being in control.

In addition to looking in control you must sound like you mean it:

- Speak clearly in a firm, steady voice.
- Use definite forms of no rather than "I don't think so," or "I probably shouldn't."
- Say it quickly—Take no longer than 30 seconds.
- Avoid debate. Say "no" however phrased, no more than twice, then get away to avoid giving the peer an opportunity to persuade.

These things give you both the look and the sound of being in control.

Discussion:

Conclude this activity by generating a discussion using the following questions:

— *In what other situations is it important to be able to say no?*
— *What does it mean to look in control?*
— *What does it mean to sound like you are in control?*
— *How does being in control make you feel about yourself?*
— *How does being in control make others feel toward you?*

Four Ways to Say NO!

Leader Presentation and Discussion

Notes:

Note: In the Activity, *Practice, Practice, Practice*, students will have an opportunity to role play refusal situations where they will be able to get experience with what is presented in this activity.

What this activity teaches:

- There are many ways to say no, and having a repertoire of ways to say no is very important..
- Being able to say no generates respect for self and the respect of others.
- Saying no is the most important skill in avoiding tobacco use.

You will need:

Whiteboard or chart pad with appropriate markers and a copy of the *Refusal Skills and Ways to Say No* experience sheet for each student

Directions:

1. Explain to the students that it is vital that they have the courage and the skills to say no when someone asks them to do something that is wrong or dangerous. It is also important to have techniques for saying no in any situation where doing so is appropriate.
2. Place the following list on the whiteboard or on your chart paper, and explain to the students that the following are four ways of saying no that will make it easier in any situation.

- **Say no.**
- **Say no, and give a reason.**
- **Say no, and suggest something else to do.**
- **Say no, and walk away.**

Notes:

3. Give each student a copy of the *Refusal Skills and Ways to Say No* experience sheet.

4. Take a few minutes to review what they learned in the previous activity, *Time to Really Say No!*

5. Next, review with the students the first part of the experience sheet, *How to Look and Sound in Control.* Discuss why looking and sounding in control is an important part of developing refusal skills.

6. Now discuss the four ways of saying no in the next part of the experience sheet. Go through the first way of saying no by explaining that to simply "Say no" effectively they must say it firmly, but politely. When saying it firmly, they should shake their heads no while saying no. Point out that there are many ways to simply say no. Go over the "Say no" examples by having the students take turns saying one of the examples. Remind them to shake their heads no while saying no.

7. Ask the students if they can think of any other examples of simply saying "No."

8. Now move on to the next way of saying no which is to "Say no, and give a reason." As before, have the students repeat an example from the list on their experience sheets. Tell them that with this method they are saying no and also giving an explanation in just a few words. Have them write in their own examples of saying no, and giving a reason at the end of this part of the experience sheet.

9. Move next to "Say no, and suggest something else to do." Again, have the students repeat an example from the list on their experience sheets. Tell them to think of things that are safe and healthy as they write in their own examples at the end of this part of the experience sheet.

10. Generally discuss the idea of saying no, and walking away. Tell the students that this last way of saying no is for use when they sense that they are in a dangerous or difficult

situation. Since this sometimes happens, it's important to have something that's effective and ready to use. The best way to handle situations like these is to "Say no, and walk away." This may take courage, but every time you do, you feel great about yourself and it becomes easier to do. When you have the feeling that you're someplace you really don't want to be, "Say no, and walk away." Stress to the students that **"If you are ever in danger, always leave. Go find someone who can help you."**

Notes:

Refusal Skills and Ways to Say No

Reminder Guide

How to Look and Sound in Control

Refusal skills help us "say no" in situations where we want to take control of how we are going to behave. In addition to saying no, we must look and sound in control to show others that we mean what we are saying. Here are two important things to help you be in control of any situation.

Your body language must communicate self-confidence, clear purpose, and control:

- Good posture with a straight back whether sitting, standing or walking.
- Face the other person and maintain eye contact.
- Look proud, strong, confident (even when not feeling much like it).

These things give you the ***look*** of being in control.

In addition to looking in control you must sound like you mean it:

- Speak clearly in a firm, steady voice.
- Use definite forms of no rather than "I don't think so," or "I probably shouldn't."
- Say it quickly—Take no longer than 30 seconds.
- Avoid debate. Say no however phrased, no more than twice, then get away to avoid giving the other person an opportunity to persuade you.

These things give you both the ***look*** and the ***sound*** of being in control.

Having the look and the sound of being in control gets you ready for what to say that will put you in control of difficult situations.

Four Ways to Say No and Mean It.

1. **Say no.**
2. **Say no, and give a reason.**
3. **Say no, and suggest something else to do.**
4. **Say no, and walk away.**

Now you'll see lots of examples of the four ways to say no. Don't stop here. Think of some ways that will work for you.

1. "Say no:"

"No."
"No way."
"Don't think I will."
"Certainly not."
"No. Not me."
"Nope."
"I'll pass."
"Un-uh."

2. "Say no, and give a reason:"

"No. I don't want to."
"No. I think that's really uncool."
"No. My parents are waiting for me."
"No. I think smoking is dumb."
"No. Not for me."
"No. I've got homework to do."
"No. I'm not interested."
"No. Tobacco is stupid!"

What is a reason you would give for not using tobacco?________________________

____

3. "Say no, and suggest something else to do:"

"No. Let's go watch a DVD instead."
"No. I'd rather shoot some hoops."
"No. We can go to my house and download some music."

What is something you would suggest doing instead of using tobacco? ____________

____

____

4. "Say no, walk away:"

This last way of saying no is for use when you sense that you are in a dangerous or difficult situation. Since this sometimes happens, it's important to have something that's effective and ready to use. The best way to handle situations like these is to **"Say no, and walk away."** This may take courage, but every time you do, you feel great about yourself, and it becomes easier to do. When you have the feeling that you're someplace you really don't want to be, **"Say no, and walk away."**

IF YOU ARE IN DANGER, ALWAYS LEAVE. GO FIND SOMEONE WHO CAN HELP YOU.

Practice, Practice, Practice

Skill Review and Development

Notes:

Note: This activity culminates a three-activity set that is designed to make kids aware of refusal skills and give them the opportunity to develop and take ownership of these skills.

What this activity teaches:

- Practice allows us to really be effective at dealing with the pressures to engage in tobacco use.
- No skill can be developed without practice.

You will need:

Each student should have a copy of the experience sheet, *Refusal Skills and Ways to Say No Reminder Guide,* from the previous activity

Directions:

1. Explain to the students that it is important to do more than to just know about refusal skills and ways of saying no. You must be able to do it. As with anything else, for a skill to really become a skill—something we can do well—we must work at it. We polish our skills when we practice them.

2. Go on to explain that when we consider the enormous hazards and the very real dangers associated with tobacco use, the time and effort we put into practicing these skills will be worth as much as almost anything we'll work at in our entire lives. Few people would trade their health for any kind of success. Most people who have achieved great success would gladly trade their success for good health. Working at honing your refusal skills is one of the best investments you'll ever make.

Notes:

3. Explain that this activity provides an opportunity to role play saying no to situations to which you specifically want to say "no."

Note: As the leader, we invite you to create role play situations that reflect the environment in which the students with whom you work are really experiencing. These environments vary so greatly that it has been our experience that those situations created by the educator working directly with the students are far more sensitive than the "one size fits all" variety that often find their way into most resources. Our challenge is for you to think of situations in which you would want your students to say no. Also keep in mind that these same refusal skills are vital in refusing drugs, alcohol, gang participation, and sexual abstinence. This practice time is where it all comes together.

4. Organize students into small groups or have them work in pairs as they role play the situation and practice their refusal skills.
5. In either case select one student to practice his or her skills and have the other student(s) play the antagonist. The role play should begin with an invitation from the antagonist to engage in some sort of tobacco use. Have the students use the language and manner of speaking that they are used to present the invitation and to shape their refusal responses.
6. Give each student a chance to practice all four ways of saying no while at the same time practicing the look and sound of being in control. This will give each student at least four opportunities to try out their skills of refusal. Be sure that the students identify the way of saying no that they are going to practice before the role play begins. Have the students refer to their experience sheet, *Refusal Skills and Ways to Say No*, as a reminder of the four ways to say "No" that they will role play.

Notes:

Note: It is also recommended that, if possible, students be given additional chances to review the refusal skill activities and engage in further practice at regular intervals throughout the year.

Discussion:

Conclude the role play activity by using the following questions to generate discussion:

— *What was it like to practice saying no?*

— *In what ways do you find it harder to say no than to say yes in these kinds of situations?*

— *Given the health consequences of tobacco use, how is being able to say no to tobacco use important to you?*

The Skill Development Game

Skill Review and Additional Practice

Notes:

Note: This activity provides additional opportunities for practicing refusal skills. It can be used to supplement previous activities or as a refresher a week or two after the *Practice, Practice, Practice* activity.

What this activity teaches:

- Acquiring any new skill takes practice.
- Being able to say no puts a person in control as opposed to being controlled.

You will need:

A copy of the experience sheet, *Saying No and Meaning It!*, for each student

Directions:

1. Explain to the students that for knowledge of a skill to really become a skill it takes practice. This activity will afford another opportunity to sharpen their refusal skills.
2. Pass out the experience sheet, *Saying No and Meaning It*, to each student.
3. Review the instructions and have the students complete each cartoon bubble. When all have finished, ask for volunteers to share some of the responses they wrote down.
4. Next, have the students form into a circle before you explain the activity. Be sure that you participate as well.
5. Explain that everyone will get a chance to participate by thinking of a new way to say no. Point out that everyone is to share a way to say no that has not been mentioned by anyone else in the circle before them. Ask the students to recall

Notes:

some of the ways of saying no they have just written down on their experience sheets or have read about or practiced in other activities. Let them know that they can really get into this practice by putting some feeling into their sharing by providing some guidelines like those that follow:

- They can say no angrily, firmly, politely, or humorously.
- They can use facial expressions; use different words, stand up, stomp their feet, shake their heads, etc.

Ask for a volunteer to begin by demonstrating a way to say "no."

6. Continue going around the circle with the sharing until everyone has run out of ideas. Be sure to take a turn also.

Discussion:

End with a discussion about the importance of developing refusal skills asking such questions as:

— *What is meant by the term "skills of refusal?"*
— *Why is it important to spend time practicing skills of refusal?*
— *Why is it hard to say no to an adult? ...To a friend? ...To a group of friends?*

Saying No and Meaning It!

There are many ways to say "No" to smoking, chewing and other dangerous things. Practice how you would say "No" by filling in the blank speech bubbles below.

Read My Lips

Skill Review and Additional Practice

Notes:

What this activity teaches:

- To be more proficient at taking charge of a situation with the effective use of refusal skills.
- To anticipate situations where saying no will be appropriate.
- Sometimes saying no takes persistence and can be a real challenge.

You will need:

Pre-prepared situation 3 x 5 cards

Directions:

Note: Before engaging students in this activity, take time to prepare at least a dozen cards with situations that you know your students are likely to encounter in their day to day environments. On each card use a sentence or two to describe the situation. A variation can be to have the students brainstorm the situations before the activity. These ideas can then be used to prepare the cards in advance of this activity. Remember these are to be situations to which the students will want to say "no."

1. Begin this activity by acknowledging that the students have now done several activities learning and practicing refusal skills; stress that in order to really learn a skill and be able to do it under pressure and stress they must practice it many times.
2. Have the students think of something that they have become good at doing. Ask them what people have to do if they want to get good at something. Once again explain that for knowledge of a skill to really become a skill it takes practice. This activity will afford additional opportunity to practice refusal skills.

3. Explain to the students that sometimes people don't accept our refusal and keep trying to convince us to do the thing we don't want to do. Additional practice is necessary to give students the confidence and skill to stay in control when others are being insistent and persuasive about doing something harmful or wrong.
4. Ask students to work in pairs, but point out that only one pair will be presenting at a time. The rest of the students will be observers.
5. Have a pair of students stand so that they will be facing each other in front of the observers. One student is to be the Convincer and the other will be the Refuser in the first round. Ask which of the students wants to be the Convincer. Draw a card with a situation on it, and give it to this student. Tell the other student that he or she will be the Refuser.
6. Tell everyone that the Convincers are to try anything to get a yes answer. The Refusers should resist verbally, with appropriate body language, and practice leaving the scene. Remind them that voice and facial expression relay a strong message when saying no. Tell them to make it short and closed to discussion. Have them use the Convincer's name to emphasize: Looking them clearly in the eye say, "No (use name)."
7. Switch roles so each gets to be the Convincer and Refuser for the same situation.
8. With each round choose a new situation card for each pair and continue the practice until every student has a chance to be both a Convincer and a Refuser.

Note: Practicing how to politely ask a person not to smoke around them is also a good skill for students to have. A discussion and practice role plays on this topic are highly recommended.

Notes:

Notes:

Discussion:

Conclude the activity with a discussion using the following questions:

— *How did you feel as the Convincer? ...Resister?*
— *Did you feel like you had to explain your reasons for saying "no"? ...If so, why?*
— *In what ways did resisting get any easier as you continued to do it?*

Saying Yes And Saying No

Experience Sheet

What this activity teaches:

- In life we get to say yes to most things which enrich our lives and that are fun and healthy.
- When it is necessary to say no, we can easily make the distinction with those things that we want in our lives.
- It is important to think about the things we want and don't want in our lives.

You will need:

One copy of the experience sheet, *Saying Yes and Saying No*, for each student

Directions:

1. Talk with the students about how each person is an individual with unique likes and dislikes, and wants and don't wants.
2. Tell them that in this activity they will have a chance to look at the things they like and want to have in their lives and other things that they don't want in their lives and to which they will want and need to say no.
3. Give each student a copy of the *Saying Yes and Saying No* experience sheet which follows this activity. Ask them to take a few minutes to fill in the blanks and respond to the questions.
4. When the students have had time to complete their experience sheets, have them gather in a circle.
5. Explain to them that we often know about the things we like and dislike, but don't have too much opportunity to discover what the things others like and dislike are. Tell them that one

Notes:

Notes:

way to learn more about one another is to share the things we like and don't like.

6. To facilitate this sharing, explain that anyone who would like can share some of the likes and dislikes they wrote down on their experience sheets.. Ask everyone to just listen to the person who is sharing without asking questions or interrupting.
7. Ask the students who would like to begin. After each student who wishes to share has done so, invite someone else to share by asking, *Who would like to go next?* You may also want to take a turn and share some of your own likes and dislikes.
8. Provide enough time for everyone who wishes to share to do so.

Discussion:

After everyone who would like has shared, facilitate a discussion with the following questions:

— *What is it about some things that make them things you like? ...Dislike?*
— *How does being able to say no to the things you don't want to do, or have in your lives make you feel?*
— *When you find yourself doing things you like, how does it make you feel?*
— *When you find yourself doing something you don't like or know you shouldn't be doing, how does that feel?*

Saying Yes and Saying No

Things That Make Me, ME

Part of what makes me ME are the things I Like and don't like. I can easily say YES to my favorite things. This is a list of my favorites; things I say yes to:

Musical group: ______________________________

Holiday: ______________________________

Restaurant: ______________________________

TV show: ______________________________

Comic/cartoon: ______________________________

Amusement park: ______________________________

Movie: ______________________________

Song: ______________________________

Food: ______________________________

Some things bother me, and I don't like them. I don't want them in my life so it is easy for me to say NO to this list: ______________________________

____

____

I really don't like it when ______________________________

____

When I am saying no to the things I don't like and don't want in my life, I have more time for the things I really want in my life.

When I am doing things I like, I feel ______________________________

____

When I am able to say NO to the things I don't like, I feel ______________________________

____

What I Know About Refusal Skills and Taking Control

Learning Evaluation

Notes:

Note: This activity may be used before you begin this section to see where students are with their prior knowledge and then again after they have participated in the activities in this section. This pre- post evaluation is useful to gauge student progress and learning acquisition. Be sure to collect the completed Learning Summaries from the pre-evaluation so that you and the students can compare them to the post-evaluation.

What this activity teaches:

- Media influence is broad and pervasive..
- Through careful manipulation and without knowing its power, media can persuade us to begin using tobacco products.

You will need:

Copies of the two-page Learning Summary, *What I Know About Refusal Skills and Taking Control*, for each student

Directions:

1. Acknowledge the students for the work they have done in completing the activities that help them understand the power of media influence as the tobacco industry tries to turn young people into users.
2. Now that the students have completed these activities it is a good time to see what they have learned. To accomplish this you can ask them to complete the *What I Know About Refusal Skills and Taking Control* Learning Summary.

3. Pass out one Learning Summary set to each student. Review the instructions for both parts of the summary with the students and make sure they understand how to proceed. Provide them enough time to complete the summary (about ten minutes).
4. After they have completed the exercise, you may gather the completed summaries for review and correction, or you may let the students self-correct their summaries.
5. Review the answers to each question with the students and answer any questions they may have. If you had the students complete the Learning Summaries before you began the activities in this section, hand out the initial evaluations and let the students see the differences in their scores.
6. Conclude the activity by again acknowledging the students for their efforts.

Notes:

Answer Key:

Part I	**Part II**
1. True	1. reason
2. False	2. courage
3. True	3. control
4. True	4. practice
5. False	5. confident
6. True	6. unique

Four Ways to Say "No:"

1. Say "No." (Just say "No.")
2. Say "No," and give a reason.
3. Say "No," and suggest something else to do.
4. Say "No," and walk away.

What I Know About Refusal Skills and Taking Control

Part I.

At the end of each sentence, write the word "True" if you think it is correct, or write the word "False" if you think it is incorrect.

1. Knowing how to use refusal skills is important in all parts of life. ____________
2. When saying "No" to something you don't want to do, it is not important to look and sound in control. ____________
3. When saying "No" to something you don't want to do, it is important to speak clearly in a firm, steady voice. ____________
4. It's important to practice techniques for saying "No" so you'll be prepared and know what to do in any situation where you need to say "No." ____________
5. When Saying "No" to someone, it's okay to also be rude about it. ____________
6. If you feel like you might be in danger, immediately walk away and find someone who can help you. ____________

Part II.

Complete each sentence by writing the correct word from the following word list in the blank space.

(confident, control, reason, unique, practice, courage)

1. Of the many ways to say "No." One is to say "No" and give a _________________.
2. It takes ___________________ to walk away from a dangerous situation.
3. Looking and sounding in ___________________ is an important part of developing refusal skills.

4. If you want to be really good at something, you must ___________________.

5. The more you practice refusal skills the more ___________________ you become.

6. It's important to remember that each person is ___________________ with individual likes and dislikes, wants and don't wants.

In the space below list the Four Ways to Say "No:"

1. ____

2. ____

3. ____

4. ____

Appendix

The following information has been extracted from the Executive Summary of the 2004 Surgeon General's Report (SGR) on tobacco use. It represents the most recent conclusions of the devastating and far reaching impact that tobacco has on human health. Most striking is that tobacco use has adverse and harmful effects on virtually every part of the body, and these effects are the most significant contributors to premature death among all public health concerns. It is safe to say that smoking and other tobacco use is tantamount to playing Russian Roulette or engaging in a prolonged effort at committing suicide while often simultaneously poisoning those around us.

The Executive Summary makes a compelling comparison between conclusions from earlier SGRs and those reported in 2004. The table presents three columns. The first is the disease being referred to in columns two and three. The second column contains conclusions from earlier SGRs with the year of the report in parentheses. The third column contains the latest conclusions regarding diseases and other adverse health effects resulting from tobacco use and specifically smoking.

To access this information go to the following Web site:

<http://www.cdc.gov/tobacco/sgr/sgr_2004/index.htm>

Diseases and other adverse health effects for which smoking is identified as a cause in the current Surgeon General's report

Disease	Highest level conclusion from previous Surgeon General's reports (year)	Conclusion from the 2004 Surgeon General's report
Cancer		
Bladder cancer	"Smoking is a cause of bladder cancer; cessation reduces risk by about 50 percent after only a few years, in comparison with continued smoking." (1990, p. 10)	"The evidence is sufficient to infer a causal relationship between smoking and. . .bladder cancer."
Cervical cancer	"Smoking has been consistently associated with an increased risk for cervical cancer." (2001, p. 224)	"The evidence is sufficient to infer a causal relationship between smoking and cervical cancer."
Esophageal cancer	"Cigarette smoking is a major cause of esophageal cancer in the United States." (1982, p. 7)	"The evidence is sufficient to infer a causal relationship between smoking and cancers of the esophagus."
Kidney cancer	"Cigarette smoking is a contributory factor in the development of kidney cancer in the United States. The term 'contributory factor' by no means excludes the possibility of a causal role for smoking in cancers of this site." (1982, p. 7)	"The evidence is sufficient to infer a causal relationship between smoking and renal cell, [and] renal pelvis... cancers."
Laryngeal cancer	"Cigarette smoking is causally associated with cancer of the lung, larynx, oral cavity, and esophagus in women as well as in men...." (1980, p. 126)	"The evidence is sufficient to infer a causal relationship between smoking and cancer of the larynx."
Leukemia	"Leukemia has recently been implicated as a smoking-related disease… but this observation has not been consistent." (1990, p. 176)	"The evidence is sufficient to infer a causal relationship between smoking and acute myeloid leukemia."
Lung cancer	"Additional epidemiological, pathological, and experimental data not only confirm the conclusion of the Surgeon General's 1964 Report regarding lung cancer in men but strengthen the causal relationship of smoking to lung cancer in women." (1967, p. 36)	"The evidence is sufficient to infer a causal relationship between smoking and lung cancer."
Oral cancer	"Cigarette smoking is a major cause of cancers of the oral cavity in the United States." (1982, p. 6)	"The evidence is sufficient to infer a causal relationship between smoking and cancers of the oral cavity and pharynx."

Disease	Highest level conclusion from previous Surgeon General's reports (year)	Conclusion from the 2004 Surgeon General's report
Pancreatic cancer	**"Smoking cessation reduces the risk of pancreatic cancer, compared with continued smoking, although this reduction in risk may only be measurable after 10 years of abstinence." (1990, p. 10)**	**"The evidence is sufficient to infer a causal relationship between smoking and pancreatic cancer."**
Stomach cancer	**"Data on smoking and cancer of the stomach. . .are unclear." (2001, p. 231)**	**"The evidence is sufficient to infer a causal relationship between smoking and gastric cancers."**
Cardiovascular diseases		
Abdominal aortic aneurysm	"Death from rupture of an atherosclerotic abdominal aneurysm is more common in cigarette smokers than in nonsmokers." (1983, p. 195)	"The evidence is sufficient to infer a causal relationship between smoking and abdominal aortic aneurysm."
Atherosclerosis	"Cigarette smoking is the most powerful risk factor predisposing to atherosclerotic peripheral vascular disease." (1983, p. 8)	"The evidence is sufficient to infer a causal relationship between smoking and subclinical atherosclerosis."
Cerebrovascular disease	"Cigarette smoking is a major cause of cerebrovascular disease (stroke), the third leading cause of death in the United States." (1989, p. 12)	"The evidence is sufficient to infer a causal relationship between smoking and stroke."
Coronary heart disease	"In summary, for the purposes of preventive medicine, it can be concluded that smoking is causally related to coronary heart disease for both men and women in the United States." (1979, p. 1-15)	"The evidence is sufficient to infer a causal relationship between smoking and coronary heart disease."
Respiratory diseases		
Chronic obstructive pulmonary disease	"Cigarette smoking is the most important of the causes of chronic bronchitis in the United States, and increases the risk of dying from chronic bronchitis." (1964, p. 302)	"The evidence is sufficient to infer a causal relationship between active smoking and chronic obstructive pulmonary disease morbidity and mortality."
Pneumonia	**"Smoking cessation reduces rates of respiratory symptoms such as cough, sputum production, and wheezing, and respiratory infections such as bronchitis and pneumonia, compared with continued smoking." (1990, p. 11)**	"The evidence is sufficient to infer a causal relationship between smoking and acute respiratory illnesses, including pneumonia, in persons without underlying smoking-related chronic obstructive lung disease."

Disease	Highest level conclusion from previous Surgeon General's reports (year)	Conclusion from the 2004 Surgeon General's report
Respiratory effects in utero	"In utero exposure to maternal smoking is associated with reduced lung function among infants...." (2001, p. 14)	"The evidence is sufficient to infer a causal relationship between maternal smoking during pregnancy and a reduction of lung function in infants."
Respiratory effects in childhood and adolescence	"Cigarette smoking during childhood and adolescence produces significant health problems among young people, including cough and phlegm production, an increased number and severity of respiratory illnesses, decreased physical fitness, an unfavorable lipid profile, and potential retardation in the rate of lung growth and the level of maximum lung function." (1994, p. 41)	"The evidence is sufficient to infer a causal relationship between active smoking and impaired lung growth during childhood and adolescence." "The evidence is sufficient to infer a causal relationship between active smoking and the early onset of lung function decline during late adolescence and early adulthood. " "The evidence is sufficient to infer a causal relationship between active smoking and respiratory symptoms in children and adolescents, including coughing, phlegm, wheezing, and dyspnea." "The evidence is sufficient to infer a causal relationship between active smoking and asthma-related symptoms (i.e., wheezing) in childhood and adolescence."
Respiratory effects in adulthood	"Cigarette smoking accelerates the age-related decline in lung function that occurs among never smokers. With sustained abstinence from smoking, the rate of decline in pulmonary function among former smokers returns to that of never smokers." (1990, p. 11)	"The evidence is sufficient to infer a causal relationship between active smoking in adulthood and a premature onset of and an accelerated age-related decline in lung function." "The evidence is sufficient to infer a causal relationship between sustained cessation from smoking and a return of the rate of decline in pulmonary function to that of persons who had never smoked."

Disease	Highest level conclusion from previous Surgeon General's reports (year)	Conclusion from the 2004 Surgeon General's report
Other respiratory effects	"Smoking cessation reduces rates of respiratory symptoms such as cough, sputum production, and wheezing, and respiratory infections such as bronchitis and pneumonia, compared with continued smoking." (1990, p. 11)	"The evidence is sufficient to infer a causal relationship between active smoking and all major respiratory symptoms among adults, including coughing, phlegm, wheezing, and dyspnea." "The evidence is sufficient to infer a causal relationship between active smoking and poor asthma control."
Reproductive effects		
Fetal death and stillbirths	"The risk for perinatal mortality—both stillbirth and neonatal deaths—and the risk for sudden infant death syndrome (SIDS) are increased among the offspring of women who smoke during pregnancy." (2001, p. 307)	"The evidence is sufficient to infer a causal relationship between sudden infant death syndrome and maternal smoking during and after pregnancy."
Fertility	"Women who smoke have increased risks for conception delay and for both primary and secondary infertility." (2001, p. 307)	"The evidence is sufficient to infer a causal relationship between smoking and reduced fertility in women."
Low birth weight	"Infants born to women who smoke during pregnancy have a lower average birth weight. . .than...infants born to women who do not smoke." (2001, p. 307)	"The evidence is sufficient to infer a causal relationship between maternal active smoking and fetal growth restriction and low birth weight."
Pregnancy complications	"Smoking during pregnancy is associated with increased risks for preterm premature rupture of membranes, abruptio placentae, and placenta previa, and with a modest increase in risk for preterm delivery." (2001, p. 307)	"The evidence is sufficient to infer a casual relationship between maternal active smoking and premature rupture of the membranes, placenta previa, and placental abruption." "The evidence is sufficient to infer a causal relationship between maternal active smoking and preterm delivery and shortened gestation."

Disease	Highest level conclusion from previous Surgeon General's reports (year)	Conclusion from the 2004 Surgeon General's report
Other effects		
Cataract	"Women who smoke have an increased risk for cataract." (2001, p. 331)	"The evidence is sufficient to infer a causal relationship between smoking and nuclear cataract."
Diminished health status/morbidity	"Relationships between smoking and cough or phlegm are strong and consistent; they have been amply documented and are judged to be causal...." (1984, p. 47) "Consideration of evidence from many different studies has led to the conclusion that cigarette smoking is the overwhelmingly most important cause of cough, sputum, chronic bronchitis, and mucus hypersecretion." (1984, p. 48)	"The evidence is sufficient to infer a causal relationship between smoking and diminished health status that may be manifest as increased absenteeism from work and increased use of medical care services." "The evidence is sufficient to infer a causal relationship between smoking and increased risks for adverse surgical outcomes related to wound healing and respiratory complications."
Hip fractures	"Women who currently smoke have an increased risk for hip fracture compared with women who do not smoke." (2001, p. 321)	"The evidence is sufficient to infer a causal relationship between smoking and hip fractures."
Low bone density	"Postmenopausal women who currently smoke have lower bone density than do women who do not smoke." (2001, p. 321)	"In postmenopausal women, the evidence is sufficient to infer a causal relationship between smoking and low bone density."
Peptic ulcer disease	"The relationship between cigarette smoking and death rates from peptic ulcer, especially gastric ulcer, is confirmed. In addition, morbidity data suggest a similar relationship exists with the prevalence of reported disease from this cause." (1967, p. 40)	"The evidence is sufficient to infer a causal relationship between smoking and peptic ulcer disease in persons who are Helicobacter pylori positive."

Sources: U.S. Department of Health and Human Services. (2004). *The health consequences of smoking: A report of the surgeon general*. Retrieved March 11, 2005, from <http://www.cdc.gov/tobacco/sgr/sgr_2004/index.htm>